# PYTHON PROGRAMMING

"The ultimate guide to programming with Python! The best coding tips to achieve an excellent level of proficiency. Accelerated intensive course, in one week! Discover the secrets and learn Python programming through various exercises with their solutions!"

*Philip Better*

© Copyright 2024 by Philip Better - All rights reserved.

The following Book is reproduced below with the goal of providing information that is as accurate and reliable as possible. Regardless, purchasing this Book can be seen as consent to the fact that both the publisher and the author of this book are in no way experts on the topics discussed within and that any recommendations or suggestions that are made herein are for entertainment purposes only. Professionals should be consulted as needed prior to undertaking any of the action endorsed herein.

This declaration is deemed fair and valid by both the American Bar Association and the Committee of Publishers Association and is legally binding throughout the United States.

Furthermore, the transmission, duplication, or reproduction of any of the following work including specific information will be considered an illegal act irrespective of if it is done electronically or in print. This extends to creating a secondary or tertiary copy of the work or a recorded copy and is only allowed with the express written consent from the Publisher. All additional right reserved.

The information in the following pages is broadly considered a truthful and accurate account of facts and as such, any inattention, use, or misuse of the information in question by the reader will render any resulting actions solely under their purview. There are no scenarios in which the publisher or the original author of this work can be in any fashion deemed liable for any hardship or damages that may befall them after undertaking information described herein.

Additionally, the information in the following pages is intended only for informational purposes and should thus be thought of as universal. As befitting its nature, it is presented without assurance regarding its prolonged validity or interim quality. Trademarks that are mentioned are done without written consent and can in no way be considered an endorsement from the trademark holder.

# Table Of Content

**INTRODUCTION** .................................................................................... 8

**CHAPTER 1: WELCOME TO PYTHON** ................................................. 10
- Introduction to Python Programming .......................................... 10
- The Evolution and Popularity of Python ...................................... 13
- Setting Up Python: Installation and Configuration .................... 16
- Your First Python Program: Hello, World! ................................... 20

**CHAPTER 2: PYTHON BASICS** ............................................................ 26
- Understanding Python Syntax ...................................................... 27
- Variables and Data Types ............................................................. 29
- Basic Python Operators ................................................................ 33
- Input and Output Operations ....................................................... 37
- Exercises: Practicing Python Basics ............................................. 40

**CHAPTER 3: CONTROL FLOW IN PYTHON** ....................................... 43
- Implementing Conditional Statements (If, Elif, Else) ................. 43
- Introduction to Loops (For and While) ........................................ 46
- Controlling Program Flow with Break and Continue ................. 48
- Exercises: Building Control Structures ........................................ 51

**CHAPTER 4: DATA STRUCTURES: ORGANIZING DATA EFFECTIVELY** ......... 55
- Lists: Managing Ordered Data ...................................................... 56
- Tuples and Their Immutable Nature ............................................ 58
- Exploring Dictionaries for Key-Value Pairing ............................. 61
- Sets and Their Operations ............................................................ 63
- Exercises: Data Structures Manipulation .................................... 66

**CHAPTER 5: FUNCTIONS: MODULARIZING YOUR CODE** ................ 70
- Defining Functions and Understanding Scope ........................... 71
- Parameters, Arguments, and Return Values ............................... 73
- Anonymous Functions: Lambda Expressions ............................. 75
- Exercises: Designing and Using Functions .................................. 78

**CHAPTER 6: STRING MASTERY IN PYTHON** ..................................... 81
- Basic String Operations and Formatting ..................................... 82
- Advanced String Methods ............................................................. 84
- Regular Expressions for Pattern Searching ................................. 86
- Exercises: String Processing Challenges ..................................... 89

**CHAPTER 7: FILE I/O: READING AND WRITING FILES** ..................... 93
- Opening and Reading Files .......................................................... 93

Writing and Appending to Files ................................................................. 96
  Handling Different File Formats (Text, CSV, JSON) ........................................ 98
  Exercises: File Handling Scenarios ............................................................. 100

## CHAPTER 8: ERROR HANDLING: MAKING YOUR CODE BULLETPROOF ..... 104

  Basics of Error and Exception Handling ...................................................... 105
  Using Try, Except, Finally Blocks ............................................................... 107
  Creating Custom Exceptions ..................................................................... 109
  Exercises: Implementing Robust Error Handling ........................................... 111

## CHAPTER 9: MODULES AND PACKAGES: EXPANDING YOUR TOOLBOX ..... 115

  Using Built-in Modules ............................................................................ 116
  Installing and Importing External Packages ................................................. 118
  Organizing Your Code with Custom Modules ................................................ 120
  Exercises: Working with Modules and Packages ........................................... 123

## CHAPTER 10: DIVING INTO OBJECT-ORIENTED PROGRAMMING ................ 126

  Understanding Classes and Objects ............................................................ 127
  Inheritance: Extending Classes .................................................................. 129
  Encapsulation and Abstraction Concepts ..................................................... 131
  Exercises: Object-Oriented Design and Implementation ................................. 134

## CHAPTER 11: ADVANCED TOPICS IN PYTHON ................................................ 137

  Decorators: Enhancing Functionality .......................................................... 138
  Iterators and Generators .......................................................................... 140
  Comprehensions for Efficient Data Processing ............................................. 142
  Context Managers for Resource Management .............................................. 144
  Exercises: Advanced Python Coding Challenges ........................................... 148

## CHAPTER 12: WEB DEVELOPMENT BASICS WITH PYTHON ......................... 151

  Introduction to Web Frameworks (Flask, Django) .......................................... 152
  Building Your First Web Application ........................................................... 153
  Templates, Routing, and Web Forms ........................................................... 156
  Exercises: Creating Basic Web Applications ................................................. 159

## CHAPTER 13: PYTHON FOR DATA SCIENCE AND MACHINE LEARNING ...... 163

  Data Analysis with Pandas ........................................................................ 164
  Data Visualization: Matplotlib and Seaborn ................................................. 167
  Introduction to Machine Learning with Scikit-Learn ..................................... 169
  Exercises: Data Science Mini-Projects ........................................................ 173

## CHAPTER 14: THE ROAD AHEAD: BECOMING A PYTHON EXPERT ............. 176

  Exploring Further: Advanced Libraries and Frameworks ................................ 176
  Community Engagement and Open-Source Contributions .............................. 179

CAREER OPPORTUNITIES AND CONTINUOUS LEARNING ............................................................. 181
EXERCISES: COMPREHENSIVE CAPSTONE PROJECTS ............................................................... 185
## APPENDIX ..................................................................................................... 189
PYTHON GLOSSARY ................................................................................................... 189
FURTHER LEARNING RESOURCES ................................................................................. 192
ACKNOWLEDGMENTS AND CONTRIBUTOR NOTES ........................................................... 195
## BONUS ............................................................................................................ 198

# Introduction

Welcome to the enthralling world of Python programming! As you embark on this chapter, "Welcome to Python," prepare to immerse yourself in an adventure that will transform the way you think about and interact with technology. Python is not just a programming language; it's a gateway to a realm where creativity and logic intertwine to bring ideas to life. This chapter is like the first step on a really cool adventure that will make you feel smart and strong.

We start by introducing you to Python programming, shedding light on the elegance and simplicity that make Python an exceptional language for beginners and seasoned developers alike. You'll explore the fascinating evolution of Python, understanding how it emerged from a single individual's vision to become one of the most popular and versatile languages in the tech world. The journey then takes you through the crucial steps of setting up Python, preparing your computer to become the canvas for your coding creations. Finally, we celebrate the rite of passage for every new programmer: writing your first Python program, "Hello, World!" This iconic initiation will mark the beginning of your beautiful relationship with Python programming.

# Chapter 1: Welcome to Python

# Introduction to Python Programming

Embarking on the journey of Python programming is akin to discovering a new world of possibilities in the realm of technology and creativity. Python, with its elegant syntax and powerful capabilities, stands as a beacon for beginners and experienced developers alike, offering a platform where simplicity meets sophistication.

Python's genesis, attributed to Guido van Rossum in the late 1980s, was driven by a desire to create a language that embraced readability and user-friendliness, without sacrificing the power and flexibility needed for complex software development. Python has become really popular and can be used for many different things. Its applications range from simple task automation to driving the backbone of web applications and even fueling scientific research that pushes the boundaries of our understanding.

One of the foundational elements of Python is its readability. When you write Python code, it's almost like drafting a piece of literature. The strict emphasis on formatting and whitespace, rather than cluttering the code with braces and semicolons, makes it a delight to read and understand. This readability not only aids in learning but also in collaborating. Imagine a world where your code is as understandable as your native tongue – that's the world Python invites you to.

Furthermore, Python is a high-level language, meaning it abstracts the complexities of the computer's inner workings. You don't have to manage memory or delve into the nuances of how your computer processes your commands at a machine level. Python allows you to concentrate on what you want to do with your code instead of worrying about other things. This feature democratizes programming, making it accessible to a wider audience beyond those who have a background in computer science.

Python is very popular because it can be used for many different things. Python is a computer programming language that can help you do lots of different things on the internet. You can use it to make websites, analyze data, create artificial intelligence, and even make video games. Python has special tools and libraries that make it easy to do all these different things. Libraries like Django and Flask for web development, Pandas and NumPy for data analysis, TensorFlow and PyTorch for machine learning, and Pygame for game development are just the tip of the iceberg in Python's expansive ecosystem.

A unique aspect of Python is its community. The people in the Python community are very friendly and helpful. Newcomers find a wealth of resources, forums, and local user groups, offering a nurturing environment to learn and grow. This community doesn't just provide technical support; it fosters innovation and collaboration, encouraging members to contribute to open-source projects, share knowledge, and continuously improve the language and its ecosystem. The success of Python is as much a testament to its community as it is to its technical capabilities.

Now, let's see how Python is used in real life and how it can be helpful. Consider a simple task like data analysis. In many programming languages, this would require extensive setup and boilerplate code. Python, on the other hand, lets you dive straight into the heart of the matter with a few lines of code. By importing a library like Pandas, you can read, manipulate, and analyze complex datasets with ease and intuitiveness that is unparalleled.

Python's design philosophy, encapsulated in the Zen of Python, highlights the essence of the language. This means that things should be made in a simple way that is easy to understand. There should be only one way to do something, and it should be easy to figure out.' This philosophy guides Python developers to create clear and logical code, making it an excellent language for educational purposes and professional development alike.

Additionally, Python is a type of computer language that can understand and follow instructions right away without needing to go through a special process called compiling. This feature enhances the learning experience, as it allows for immediate feedback and a more interactive approach to coding. You write, you run, you see the results – it's a seamless loop of learning and improvement.

In the realm of software development, Python is often chosen for its efficiency and effectiveness. It enables developers to write less code compared to other languages like C++ or Java, yet achieve the same, or even greater functionality. This efficiency translates into faster development times, making Python an ideal choice for startups and tech companies that need to move quickly and adapt to changing market demands.

Python is also really good for learning things in school. Its straightforward syntax and readability make it an excellent first language for students venturing into programming. The skills learned through Python are transferable to other programming languages, making it a foundational tool in the arsenal of any aspiring programmer.

To put it simply, Python is more than just a way to write computer programs. It can help you be creative, come up with new ideas, and open up lots of cool jobs for you in the future. Whether you're a hobbyist looking to automate simple tasks, a scientist conducting complex data analysis, or a developer building the next big tech solution, Python provides the tools, community, and flexibility to help you achieve your goals. As you step into the world of Python programming, remember that you're joining a global community of innovators and creators, all united by the elegant simplicity of Python.

# The Evolution and Popularity of Python

The story of Python is a fascinating journey through time, showcasing the evolution of a language that began as a humble experiment and blossomed into a cornerstone of modern software development. Its rise to popularity is not just a tale of technical prowess but also a narrative about community, adaptability, and the timeless pursuit of simplicity in the complex world of programming.

Python's inception in the late 1980s by Guido van Rossum, then a programmer at the Centrum Wiskunde & Informatica (CWI) in the Netherlands, marked the birth of a language that was set to revolutionize the way we think about software development. Van Rossum, a man with a vision to overcome the shortcomings of the ABC language, sought to create a language that emphasized code readability, simplicity, and an open-minded approach to problem-solving. The first release of Python in 1991, Python 0.9.0, introduced key features like exception handling and the core data types that form the foundation of Python today.

As Python grew and changed, it became known for being able to do many different things and being easy for people to use. In the early 2000s, a really important thing happened - a new version of a programming language called Python was released, and it was called Python 2.0. This version brought in Unicode support, a feature that broadened Python's global appeal, allowing programmers from all over the world to work in their native languages. Python 2.0 also introduced a fully garbage-collected memory management system, making the language more robust and reliable.

The journey from Python 2 to Python 3 was a pivotal moment in Python's history. Python 3.0, released in 2008, was a major leap forward, featuring improvements in the language's core and removing redundancies. This version was not backward compatible, a courageous move that epitomized Python's commitment to progress, even at the cost of short-term inconvenience. This transition period was marked by debates and uncertainty within the community, but ultimately it paved the way for a more consistent and efficient Python.

Python's way of thinking is all about keeping things simple and beautiful. This philosophy is not just evident in the syntax of the language but also in its comprehensive standard library, often referred to as Python's "batteries-included" approach. This extensive library, ranging from internet protocols to web services, data compression to cryptography, sets Python apart as a swiss army knife in a programmer's toolkit.

The rise of Python in the fields of data science and machine learning in the 2010s further cemented its position as a leader in programming languages. The creation and growth of powerful libraries like NumPy, Pandas, and Matplotlib for data analysis and manipulation, along with TensorFlow and PyTorch for machine learning, made Python an irresistible choice for scientists, researchers, and data analysts. This era marked Python's transition from a general-purpose programming language to a fundamental tool in emerging tech sectors.

Python's popularity is also deeply rooted in its community and culture. The Python community, often cited as one of the most welcoming and supportive in the tech world, has played a crucial role in its growth. Contributions from thousands of developers and enthusiasts have led to the creation of a rich ecosystem of frameworks, libraries, and tools. The community's commitment to open-source principles has allowed Python to evolve with the diverse and changing needs of programmers around the world.

In the realm of education, Python has become the go-to language for introducing students to programming. This is easy for beginners to understand because it is simple and not too hard. It helps them learn the basics of programming without getting confused by difficult words and rules. Many top universities have adopted Python as the primary language for teaching computer science and programming courses, a testament to its effectiveness as an educational tool.

The versatility of Python is evident in its wide range of applications. From web development with frameworks like Django and Flask to scripting for system automation, from desktop applications to games, Python's applicability spans across domains. This versatility has not only made Python popular among professional developers but also among hobbyists and enthusiasts who find in Python a language that can bring their creative ideas to life.

Python's influence extends beyond its technical capabilities. The language has fostered a philosophy of coding that prioritizes readability, efficiency, and a pragmatic approach to problem-solving. Python programmers are often encouraged to think about the maintainability and scalability of their code, principles that are valuable in the ever-evolving landscape of technology.

As we look to the future, Python's trajectory continues to ascend. It is becoming more and more important in new and exciting areas like robots that think, computers that learn, and working with lots of information. The language's adaptability, coupled with a strong, forward-thinking community, suggests that Python will continue to be a key player in shaping the future of technology.

The evolution of Python is a story of how a language can grow, adapt, and thrive in the fast-paced world of technology. It's a testament to the vision of its creator, the dedication of its community, and the enduring power of simplicity in complexity. As Python continues to evolve, it remains a beacon for programmers around the world, a tool for innovation, and a canvas for creativity.

# Setting Up Python: Installation and Configuration

The journey into Python programming is akin to setting out on an exciting voyage; the first step is preparing your vessel – in this case, your computer. Installing and configuring Python is your gateway into a world where ideas transform into reality through lines of code. This process, while straightforward, is crucial in laying a strong foundation for your future endeavors in programming.

Before diving into the technicalities of installation, let's take a moment to understand what Python installation entails. Essentially, installing Python means placing the Python interpreter onto your computer. This interpreter is the heart of Python programming, reading your Python code and executing it. Think of it as learning a new language; the interpreter is your translator, allowing your computer to understand and respond to your Python commands.

The beauty of Python lies in its cross-platform nature. No matter if you have a computer with Windows, MacOS, or Linux, you can easily use Python on your computer. This universality ensures that no matter your choice of tech environment, Python is always within reach.

For Windows users, the journey begins at the Python website, where the latest version of Python awaits. The installation process is a dance of a few clicks: downloading the installer, running it, and following the on-screen instructions. However, there's a subtle but crucial step that must not be overlooked – the checkbox that says "Add Python to PATH." This small act is like laying down a map for your computer, telling it where to find Python. Without this, your journey might face unnecessary detours.

MacOS users have a slightly different path. While MacOS comes with Python pre-installed, it's often an older version. As a Python adventurer, you're seeking the latest and greatest, which means downloading the newest version from the Python website. The installation is a serene flow of opening the package, and letting the guided setup do its magic.

Linux users, the tinkerers and custodians of their tech domains, have a more hands-on approach. Python often comes pre-installed, but ensuring it's the latest version involves a rendezvous with the terminal. Commands like `sudo apt-get install python3` are the incantations you utter to bring Python to life on your machine.

Once Python is installed, the next step is to verify the installation. This is like checking your equipment before a hike. You open the command prompt or terminal, type `python --version`, and there it is – the version of Python smiling back at you, confirming that you're ready to embark on your coding journey.

Configuration is the next frontier. Python, in its raw form, is powerful, but it reaches its full potential with the right setup. An Integrated Development Environment (IDE) is like a special tool that helps people write computer programs easier. It's like having a special workspace with all the tools you need to build something cool on the computer. IDEs are like your mission control for Python programming. It's like a special place where you can write, try out, and fix your computer instructions. Some programs that many people like to use for coding are PyCharm, Visual Studio Code, and Jupyter Notebooks. Each of these environments offers unique tools and interfaces, but they all share the common goal of making your Python journey more manageable and enjoyable.

Configuring Python also involves acquainting yourself with pip, Python's package manager. Imagine pip as a magic portal where thousands of Python libraries and tools are at your fingertips. Need a library for data analysis? A tool for web development? Pip is your gateway. The command `pip install library-name` is your key to unlocking these resources.

Now, let's explore the world of virtual places you can visit on a computer. In the Python odyssey, these environments are like isolated islands, each with its own unique ecosystem. Virtual environments help you keep track of the things your computer needs to run different projects, like different versions of a program called Python. This way, you can work on different projects without them getting mixed up or causing problems. This means you can have different projects with their own specific requirements, without causing conflicts between them. Setting up a virtual environment is like preparing a dedicated workspace for each of your projects, ensuring that everything you need is organized and contained.

Creating a virtual environment is a simple yet powerful process. Using tools like `venv`, you can create these isolated environments with ease. Once activated, any Python package you install will be confined to that environment, keeping your global Python space clean and orderly. This is really important when you are doing a lot of different projects or working with other people. It means that everything will work well together and be the same no matter what kind of computer or setup you are using.

As you progress in your Python journey, understanding the importance of environment variables becomes paramount. These are the signposts that guide Python on your system. Setting environment variables correctly ensures that Python knows where to look for installed libraries and how to behave in different contexts. It's like giving your Python interpreter a compass and a set of instructions, guiding it on how to navigate your system.

Another aspect of setting up Python is understanding the Python Package Index (PyPI). PyPI is like a big library where you can find lots of different computer programs that are made for a special language called Python. Think of it as a vast library where thousands of books (in this case, Python packages) are available for you to peruse and use. It's an invaluable resource, offering tools and libraries for just about any task you can imagine in Python.

Finally, a word about staying updated. The world of Python is ever-evolving, with new versions and improvements being released regularly. When you keep your Python installation updated, it means you have the most recent version of Python. This is important because it gives you access to new and improved features, fixes any security issues, and makes Python run faster. It's like keeping your ship sea-worthy and ready to sail the latest currents of the Python seas. Updating Python, however, should be a thoughtful process, especially if you're working on critical projects. New versions might introduce changes that could affect your existing code, so it's always good to read the release notes and test your projects with the new version in a separate environment before fully committing.

In the grand tapestry of Python programming, setting up your environment is both an art and a science. It requires a blend of following instructions and understanding the landscape you're operating in. Your setup is your personal workshop, a space where your tools are arranged just the way you like, allowing you to focus on the craft of coding.

As you complete this initial setup, remember that it's more than just a series of downloads and installations. You're building a foundation for your future projects, experiments, and innovations. Every time you do one of these steps, you are getting better and better at Python programming. You're not just installing software; you're setting the stage for countless adventures in coding, each with its own challenges, learnings, and triumphs.

When you have Python set up on your computer, it's like opening a door to a huge world full of exciting things you can do. Whether it's developing sophisticated software, automating mundane tasks, analyzing data to uncover insights, or creating something entirely new, Python is your vessel, and the vast ocean of programming lies ahead, waiting for you to explore. So, take a deep breath, and prepare to dive into the exhilarating world of Python programming, where each line of code you write is a stroke of your oar, propelling you forward in this vast and wondrous sea.

# Your First Python Program: Hello, World!

There is a profound beauty in beginnings. The very beginning is like the first word you say or the first sound you make. In the world of programming, this beginning is often marked by a simple, yet powerful phrase: "Hello, World!" This tradition, spanning across various programming languages, is more than just a ritual; it's a rite of passage for every aspiring programmer, marking the start of a journey into the vast universe of coding. In Python, crafting your first "Hello, World!" program is not just an exercise in syntax, but an invitation to a world where simplicity and power coexist harmoniously.

The "Hello, World!" program is emblematic, representing the essence of Python. It encapsulates the language's philosophy of simplicity and readability. When you write this program in Python, you're not just typing characters into a text editor; you're engaging in a conversation with your computer. It's a moment of connection between you, the programmer, and the machine, mediated by Python's clear and expressive syntax.

Let's delve into the anatomy of this simple program. The code for a "Hello, World!" program in Python is almost deceivingly straightforward. All it takes is one line: `print("Hello, World!")`. But within this line lies a universe of meaning. The `print` function is your first tool, a fundamental command in Python that outputs data to the screen. It's like your first word in a new language, a simple yet versatile expression that opens doors to more complex conversations.

The parentheses and quotation marks might seem like small details, but they're essential elements of Python's syntax, representing the structure and clarity that the language is known for. The parentheses in the `print` function are like open arms, ready to embrace whatever you wish to express. The quotation marks signify that what's enclosed within them is a string, a type of data in Python that represents text.

In this single line of code, `print("Hello, World!")`, Python introduces you to several fundamental concepts: functions, strings, and the act of passing an argument to a function. These are not just abstract ideas; they are the building blocks of every Python program you will write in the future. By starting with this simple line, you're laying the foundation for your understanding of these concepts.

But the "Hello, World!" program is more than just a syntactical exercise; it's a lesson in the iterative nature of programming. As a beginner, you might type this line into an Integrated Development Environment (IDE) or a text editor, and then run it through the Python interpreter. The first time you see "Hello, World!" appear on your screen, it's a moment of triumph. This output is the result of your command, a direct response from your computer to your instructions. It's a dialogue, the most fundamental one, between you and the machine.

This moment also serves as an introduction to the process of writing, testing, and debugging code. In the future, as your programs grow in complexity, this cycle of writing, running, and refining will become a constant companion. The "Hello, World!" program is your first step into this iterative process. It's where you learn the importance of accuracy in syntax, the value of a clear output, and the satisfaction of seeing your code come to life.

As you embark on your Python journey, the simplicity of the "Hello, World!" program remains a guiding principle. Python is renowned for its straightforward syntax and its ability to express complex ideas in a few lines of code. The power of Python is not in verbosity but in its clarity and expressiveness. As you progress, you'll find that even the most complex Python programs retain this sense of clarity and simplicity.

The "Hello, World!" program is also a reminder of the vast community you're joining. Countless programmers have begun their coding journey with these same words. It's a shared experience, a common language among developers. As you write these words, you become part of a global community of learners, enthusiasts, and professionals, all united by the power of code.

Moreover, this program is an invitation to explore. Python, with its extensive libraries and frameworks, offers a world of possibilities. From creating websites to studying data, from making things automatic to creating intelligent machines, the path that starts with saying "Hello, World!" can take you to endless places. Each new project, each new line of code, is a step further in this exploration, a deeper dive into the capabilities of Python and your potential as a programmer.

When you write your first "Hello, World!" program, you are not only learning how to use a programming language, but you are also adopting a way of thinking. It's a mindset of curiosity, exploration, and continual learning. Python is a language that evolves, and as a Python programmer, you too will evolve with it. Each new version, each new library enriches your experience and expands your horizons.

As you move forward from this point, remember the joy and simplicity of your first "Hello, World!" program. In the world of programming, where complexity can often be overwhelming, returning to the basics can provide clarity and inspiration. This program symbolizes the beginning of your journey, a journey marked by endless possibilities and continual growth.

Reflect on the journey that lies ahead. With each new concept you learn, each new program you write, you'll be building on this foundational experience. The principles of Python programming are embedded in this simple program – clarity, simplicity, and elegance. These principles will guide you as you delve deeper into more complex and sophisticated programming challenges.

As you progress, you'll find that Python's simplicity doesn't limit its power. On the contrary, it enhances it. Python is a type of computer language that is easy to understand and use. It helps you solve problems without getting confused by complicated rules. This focus on problem-solving is at the heart of Python programming. Whether you're automating a small task, analyzing a dataset, or developing a complex application, Python provides the tools and flexibility to achieve your goals.

The "Hello, World!" program is just the beginning, but its significance will resonate throughout your programming career. It's a constant reminder that no matter how complex your coding tasks become, they all start with a simple step. As you embark on this exciting journey, embrace the spirit of exploration and discovery that this program represents. Let it be a source of inspiration and a reminder of the humble beginnings from which great things can grow.

In the big story of learning how to program, "Hello, World!" is like the first sentence you learn to say. It's a simple way to start and it helps you understand how to make your computer do things. It's a declaration of your entry into the world of Python programming, a world where creativity meets logic, where challenges lead to growth, and where each line of code you write is a step towards mastering this powerful and elegant language. So, embrace this beginning with enthusiasm and look forward to the countless lines of code, projects, and achievements that will follow. Welcome to Python programming – your adventure starts here.

# Conclusion of Chapter 1: Welcome to Python

As we conclude this introductory chapter, you stand at the threshold of a new realm of possibilities. "Welcome to Python" has been more than just an introduction to a programming language; it has been the opening of a door to a world where your creative and logical potentials know no bounds. You've journeyed through the rich history and evolution of Python, understanding its place in the larger narrative of technology and innovation. You've navigated the essential setup, configuring your machine to speak the language of Python, and you've taken your first steps in coding by writing the "Hello, World!" program.

This chapter has set the foundation for your Python programming journey. As you move forward, carry with you the principles of simplicity, readability, and versatility that Python embodies. Remember the excitement of seeing your first program come to life and the sense of accomplishment in setting up your programming environment. Now you have learned the basics and have the tools to explore more about Python.

Python is more than a language; it's a community, a philosophy, and a tool for change. As you progress through the upcoming chapters, embrace the challenges and opportunities that Python programming presents. Let your curiosity guide you, your creativity inspire you, and your logic drive you. Welcome to Python – your journey into programming has just begun.

# Chapter 2: Python Basics

**Introduction to Chapter 2: Python Basics**

Welcome to the chapter where the building blocks of Python programming are unveiled – "Python Basics." This chapter is a journey into the heart of Python, revealing the foundational elements that make this language not just powerful, but also intuitive and accessible. As you embark on this exploration, you will discover the simplicity and elegance that Python offers, making it a favored choice for beginners and seasoned programmers alike.

We begin by delving into the intricacies of Python syntax, understanding how this language speaks and constructs its narratives. You'll learn about variables, the dynamic labels that store and retrieve data, and data types, the various forms that data can take in Python. Moving forward, we explore the basic Python operators, the tools that allow you to perform calculations, make decisions, and manipulate data. Then, we'll transition into the vital skills of input and output operations, the mechanisms through which Python interacts with the user and the outside world. Each section of this chapter is a step further into the world of Python, unraveling its capabilities and revealing how you can harness them to bring your programming ideas to life.

# Understanding Python Syntax

Embarking on the journey of understanding Python syntax is akin to learning the grammar of a new language. It's about understanding the rules that govern the structure of the code, the way words (or in this case, elements of code) are put together to form meaningful commands. Python, renowned for its clarity and simplicity, offers a syntax that is both intuitive and powerful, enabling you to express large-scale programming concepts in a few, readable lines.

Python syntax is often celebrated for its elegance and straightforward nature. Unlike some other programming languages that require extensive boilerplate code, Python allows you to execute complex tasks with minimal lines of code. This simplicity, however, does not detract from the language's power. The key lies in understanding how Python's syntax works - how it's structured, and how you can harness it to express your programming logic effectively.

At the heart of Python's syntax is its emphasis on readability. Python uses English keywords where other languages might use punctuation, and it has strict rules on the use of whitespace. This focus on readability means that Python code often reads like English, which is one of the reasons why it's an excellent language for beginners. The simplicity of its syntax makes it easy for newcomers to pick up and for seasoned programmers to understand at a glance.

Whitespace is a critical component of Python syntax. In many languages, code blocks are defined by brackets or other punctuation. In Python, indentation - the horizontal space to the left of your code - is what defines a block of code. This use of indentation means that Python code almost always looks clean and uncluttered. There's no jumble of brackets cluttering up the end of your functions or loops – just simple, clean lines of code, each indented to show its relationship to the rest.

Python also eschews the semicolon seen at the end of lines in many other languages. In Python, the end of a line typically signifies the end of a command, making your code less cluttered and more readable. This, however, means that you need to be more deliberate about how you structure your code. Python relies on line breaks to determine when a command has ended, so understanding how to use line continuation – when a line of code extends beyond a single line for readability or other reasons – becomes crucial. You can achieve line continuation by using a backslash (\) at the end of a line or by enclosing your expression in parentheses, brackets, or braces.

Another aspect of Python syntax that stands out is its use of colons. Colons in Python are used to introduce a new block of code, which could be a loop, a function, or a conditional statement. This is coupled with the aforementioned indentation to create a visually organized and structured block of code. When you see a colon at the end of a line, it's Python's way of telling you that everything that follows, indented, is part of a related block of code. This clear demarcation of code blocks makes Python highly readable and maintainable.

Python also adopts a unique approach to variable declaration and assignment. Unlike some languages where you must explicitly declare a variable and its type, in Python, you simply assign a value to a variable name, and Python handles the type behind the scenes. This dynamic typing makes Python flexible and easy to use, although it requires a solid understanding of how Python handles different data types to avoid unexpected behavior in your code.

Python's approach to function definition is another hallmark of its syntax. The word "def" is used to create a new function. You give the function a name and put any information it needs inside parentheses. This simplicity in defining functions underlines Python's approach to programming – making it as straightforward as possible, while still allowing for complex operations.

Error handling in Python also reflects its straightforward syntax. Python uses try-except blocks to handle errors. The readability of these blocks is emblematic of Python's overall approach – clear, logical, and focused on making the code as understandable as possible.

Furthermore, Python's syntax is extensible. The language allows for the creation of custom classes and functions, enabling programmers to define their own objects and methods in a way that's consistent with the core syntax of the language. This extensibility means that Python is not just a language but a framework for building languages – a tool that you can shape to suit your specific coding needs.

In conclusion, mastering Python syntax is about more than just learning where to put your colons and how to indent your code. It's about understanding the philosophy that underlies Python – a philosophy that values clarity, simplicity, and readability. As you become more familiar with Python's syntax, you'll find yourself thinking more clearly about your code, organizing your thoughts in a way that's logical and easy to understand. This clarity of thought is one of the great gifts of Python, and it's what makes it such a powerful tool for beginners and experts alike.

## Variables and Data Types

In the captivating world of Python programming, the concept of variables and data types is akin to the very air that breathes life into the language. They are the fundamental building blocks, the basic units that store and manipulate data, shaping the way we bring logic and ideas to life in our code. Grasping the concept of variables and data types is not just about learning the rules; it's about understanding the poetry hidden within the lines of code, the subtle dance between simplicity and functionality that Python so beautifully orchestrates.

When we talk about variables in Python, we refer to them as dynamic names bound to objects. Imagine a variable as a label attached to a box, where the box can contain different types of items – numbers, texts, lists, or even other boxes. In Python, making a variable is like giving it a name and then giving it something to hold. This act of assignment is a declaration of existence. You don't need to explicitly state the type of the variable; Python is intuitive enough to understand it from the context. It's this intuitiveness that makes Python a language that's not just powerful, but also approachable.

Let's delve into the various data types that Python handles. At the most basic level, you have the integers and floats – the numeric stalwarts. Integers are your whole numbers, the counts and tallies of programming. Floats, or floating-point numbers, bring in the decimals, allowing for precision and detail. Python handles these types with ease, making numerical operations and calculations a seamless affair.

Strings in Python are sequences of characters and are as versatile as they are essential. Whether you're crafting messages, parsing text, or managing data, strings are your go-to data type. Python treats strings with a level of flexibility that's rare – you can concatenate them, slice them, format them, and so much more. This flexibility opens a plethora of possibilities in text processing and manipulation, making Python a favorite for tasks ranging from simple logging to complex natural language processing.

Then come the lists and tuples – the collectors of Python. Lists are mutable sequences, which means you can change their content, add new elements, or remove existing ones. They are the dynamic arrays of Python, adaptable and changeable. Tuples, on the other hand, are immutable. Once you create a tuple, its content stays the same. This immutability makes tuples a reliable choice for data that needs to remain constant through the lifecycle of a program.

Dictionaries in Python are uncharted territories for the uninitiated but are in fact treasure troves of efficiency and functionality. They keep information in key-value pairs, like a secret code. This helps us organize information easily and find it quickly when we need it. Think of a dictionary like the ones you use for words. In a dictionary, you look up a word to find out what it means. In Python, dictionaries work the same way. You use a word (called a key) to find its meaning (called a value). They are ideal for handling complex data structures, offering quick access and efficient management of data.

Another interesting data type in Python is the set. Sets are collections of unique elements, much like their mathematical counterparts. They are used when the uniqueness of elements is a key factor, and they come with operations like unions, intersections, and differences, mirroring the operations you would perform on sets in mathematics. Python handles sets with an efficiency that makes operations like checking for membership or eliminating duplicates effortless.

In the Python ecosystem, the beauty lies in how these data types interact and how you can convert one type into another, a process known as type casting. Python's dynamic nature allows you to be fluid with these types, adapting them as per the needs of your program. This flexibility, however, comes with the responsibility of being clear about what type your data is at any point in your code.

The dynamic typing in Python, where the type of a variable is determined at runtime, is a double-edged sword. It provides great flexibility, allowing you to write more expressive and readable code, but it also demands a higher level of awareness from you as a programmer. You need to understand the type of data you're dealing with to avoid unexpected behavior or errors in your programs.

Understanding Python's data types also involves grasping the concept of mutability. Mutability refers to whether the value of an object can change. In Python, some things called lists can be changed. This means you can make them different without making them a completely new thing. Some things, like tuples and strings, cannot be changed once they are made. Their content stays the same and cannot be changed. This distinction is crucial when designing functions and managing data within your programs, as it affects how data is passed around and manipulated.

Python's approach to variables and data types is one of the key factors that make it such an accessible and widely-used language. It helps you to concentrate on finding a solution to the problem, instead of spending too much time on saying and organizing different types of things. However, this ease of use does not absolve you of the responsibility of understanding the implications of the different data types and how they behave.

For example, when working with integers and floats, you need to be mindful of arithmetic operations and conversions between these types. Python handles numeric conversions with ease, but being aware of these conversions is important for accurate calculations, especially when dealing with floating-point arithmetic where precision is key.

Similarly, when manipulating strings, understanding how Python handles Unicode and string encoding is vital, especially in an increasingly globalized world where your programs need to handle diverse character sets.

The real power of Python's handling of variables and data types becomes evident when dealing with more complex data structures. Lists, tuples, dictionaries, and sets each offer unique ways of organizing data, and Python provides a wealth of functions and methods to work with these types. Whether it's sorting lists, accessing dictionary values, or performing set operations, Python's standard library comes equipped with everything you need to handle these tasks with ease.

In summary, the journey through Python's variables and data types is an exploration of simplicity and power. It's about understanding how to store and manipulate data in ways that are both intuitive and effective. As you learn and practice more, you will get better at writing code that is easier to understand and works faster. You'll be able to harness the full potential of Python's flexibility, turning lines of code into elegant solutions to complex problems. This understanding is not just a technical skill; it's a step towards becoming a more effective and insightful Python programmer.

## Basic Python Operators

In the fascinating journey of Python programming, operators are the essential tools that allow us to perform various operations on data. Like the verbs in a language, they define the actions that manipulate variables and values, crafting the narrative of our code. In Python, operators are simple yet powerful, designed to be intuitive and efficient. They are the gears that drive the machinery of our programs, translating our logical thoughts into actions that the computer can execute.

Let's start by exploring arithmetic operators, the most fundamental operators that deal with basic mathematical operations. In Python, these operators are not just symbols; they are the manifestation of mathematical principles. The addition (`+`) and subtraction (`-`) operators work just as you would expect, adding and subtracting values. Multiplication (`*`) and division (`/`) also follow the intuitive understanding from basic mathematics. However, Python adds a layer of finesse to these operations. For instance, the division operator always returns a float, ensuring precision in your calculations. Additionally, there's the floor division operator (`//`), which returns the quotient without the remainder, and the modulus operator (`%`), which gives you the remainder of a division. Lastly, the exponentiation operator (`**`) raises a number to the power of another, a simple yet powerful tool in your mathematical toolkit.

Beyond arithmetic, Python introduces us to comparison operators. These operators are the judges in our code, making decisions by comparing values. The equals (`==`) and not equals (`!=`) operators assess equality and inequality, while greater than (`>`), less than (`<`), greater than or equal to (`>=`), and less than or equal to (`<=`) compare the magnitudes of values. These operators are important in telling the program what to do. They help you make choices and decide what happens next based on certain conditions.

Then come the assignment operators, the scribes of Python. The basic assignment operator (`=`) is used to assign values to variables, but Python also offers a suite of shorthand operators that combine arithmetic and assignment. For instance, `+=` adds and assigns in one step, `-=` subtracts and assigns, `*=` multiplies and assigns, and so forth. These operators make your code more concise and readable, allowing you to perform operations and update variables efficiently.

Python also boasts logical operators – `and`, `or`, and `not`. These operators are the critical thinkers, evaluating multiple conditions to guide the logic of your programs. They are the tools you use to combine simple conditions into more complex ones, crafting the logic that drives decision-making in your code.

In addition to these basic operators, Python includes bitwise operators, which operate on the binary representations of numbers. These might seem esoteric at first glance, but they are incredibly powerful, especially in lower-level programming tasks, like working with files or network protocols. They include bitwise AND (`&`), OR (`|`), XOR (`^`), NOT (`~`), left shift (`<<`), and right shift (`>>`). These operators allow you to manipulate individual bits of data, providing a level of control that's especially useful in certain specialized domains.

It's important to understand how these operators work under the hood. For instance, the bitwise AND operator (`&`) compares each bit of the number on the left of the operator to the corresponding bit of the number on the right. If both bits are 1, the resulting bit is 1; otherwise, it's 0. This might seem like a detail reserved for computer scientists, but in Python, it's made accessible and usable for a wide range of applications.

Python's approach to operators is deeply rooted in the philosophy of making complex things simple. It abstracts away the intricacies of low-level data manipulation, presenting you with a set of tools that are both powerful and easy to use. This approach is evident in Python's handling of more abstract types of operators, like identity operators (`is`, `is not`) and membership operators (`in`, `not in`). These operators allow you to test for the identity of objects (whether two variables point to the same object) and membership in sequences like lists and strings, respectively.

The identity operators, particularly, shed light on Python's handling of objects and memory. When you use `is`, Python doesn't just compare values; it compares the identities of the objects involved. It's important to know the difference between how Python handles memory and stores information, especially when it comes to things that can change, like lists.

Membership operators are like the search tools in Python, checking for the presence of an element in a sequence. Their beauty lies in their simplicity and readability. A statement like `if element in my list:` reads almost like English and is a testament to Python's design, which emphasizes code readability.

When working with these operators, it's also important to understand operator precedence, which determines the order in which operations are carried out. In Python, as in mathematics, certain operations take precedence over others. Think of it like this: when you have a math problem with different operations like adding, subtracting, multiplying, or dividing, you need to do the multiplication or division parts first before you can do the addition or subtraction parts. It's like a rule that tells you which parts to do first. It's really important to know this order of importance for writing Python code that works correctly and quickly, especially when the code gets complicated.

Python's operators are more than just tools for computation; they are part of the language's commitment to clear, concise, and intuitive coding. They enable you to express complex operations in a way that is both straightforward and elegant. As you become more familiar with these operators, you'll find that they greatly enhance the expressiveness of your code, allowing you to write programs that are not just functional, but also clear and easy to understand.

In summary, the journey through Python's basic operators is an exploration of the language's ability to simplify complexity. Whether you're performing mathematical calculations, comparing values, making decisions based on conditions, or manipulating data at the bit level, Python provides you with a set of operators that are powerful yet intuitive. These operators are the fundamental tools that you will use to construct the logic of your programs, to make decisions, and to manipulate data. They are an essential part of the Python language, and understanding them is key to becoming a proficient Python programmer.

# Input and Output Operations

In the world of Python programming, mastering input and output operations is akin to learning the art of conversation. It's a dance between the program and its user, a fundamental aspect that brings interactivity and life to the lines of code. This section delves into the essence of these operations, exploring how Python not only speaks but also listens, making your programs not just a set of instructions, but a dynamic interaction.

Output in Python is predominantly handled by the `print()` function, a versatile tool that serves as the voice of your program. Every time you invoke `print()`, your program reaches out to the world, conveying information, be it a simple message, the result of a computation, or the contents of a data structure. This function is the bridge between the inner workings of your code and the outside world. But `print()` is more than just a way to show information; it's a window into your program, providing insights into its state and behavior. It's an essential tool for debugging, allowing you to peek into the execution of your program and understand how data is being manipulated.

The power of `print()` extends beyond just displaying messages. Python's string formatting capabilities transform `print()` into a dynamic storytelling tool. Whether it's through concatenation, the `str.format()` method, or formatted string literals (f-strings), Python offers a plethora of ways to weave variables into your output strings. This flexibility lets you make things that are fun and easy to use, as well as helpful and interesting.

On the other side of the conversation is input, primarily handled by the `input()` function in Python. This function is the ear of your program, allowing it to listen to the user's responses. When `input()` is called, Python pauses and waits for the user to type something into the console. Upon pressing enter, the entered text is sent back to the program as a string. This simple mechanism opens up a world of possibilities, from asking the user for their name to receiving complex data for processing.

Understanding input operations also involves recognizing Python's treatment of all inputs as strings. This characteristic means that any data you receive via `input()` needs to be converted into the appropriate type before it can be used for numerical operations or data processing. This conversion is a critical step, ensuring that the data you work with aligns with your program's expectations and requirements.

Moreover, input and output operations in Python are not limited to text. Python offers extensive support for reading from and writing to files, allowing your programs to interact with data stored on disk. This capability extends the conversation beyond the immediate interaction in the console, enabling your programs to remember past interactions, analyze large datasets, and even communicate with other programs.

Working with files in Python is made easy and intuitive thanks to its built-in functions like `open()`, `read()`, `write()`, and `close()`. These functions allow you to handle files with a level of simplicity and elegance, characteristic of Python's design philosophy. Whether it's reading configuration files, writing logs, or processing external datasets, file handling in Python is an essential skill in your programming toolkit.

But input and output operations in Python go even beyond the standard input-output and file handling. Python's extensive standard library includes modules for handling Internet data, binary data, compressed files, and various data formats. This vast array of tools further expands the ways in which your Python programs can communicate with the world, making them not just isolated scripts but connected, interactive entities.

In conclusion, input and output operations in Python form the core of program-user interaction. They transform your scripts from static sets of instructions into dynamic, responsive entities capable of engaging with users and external data sources. Mastering these operations is not just about learning the functions and syntax; it's about understanding the art of conversation in the realm of programming. As you become proficient in these skills, your Python programs will become more engaging, versatile, and powerful, capable of interacting with the world in myriad ways.

**Conclusion of Chapter 2: Python Basics**

As we conclude this chapter, you have now traversed the foundational landscape of Python. You've gained insights into the fundamental aspects that make up a Python program, from the way it's structured to how it processes and responds to information. This journey through "Python Basics" has equipped you with the essential tools and knowledge to start building your own Python programs.

Looking back, you've learned the significance of Python syntax, the backbone of your code's structure and readability. You've explored variables and data types, understanding how Python stores and categorizes data. The exploration of basic Python operators has opened your eyes to the numerous possibilities of data manipulation. Finally, mastering input and output operations has taught you how to make your programs interactive and dynamic.

As you move forward, remember that these basics are just the starting point. The journey ahead is filled with more complex concepts and exciting challenges. Python is a language that grows with you, offering more depth and capabilities as you delve deeper into its features. You are now ready to take the next steps in your Python programming journey, armed with the knowledge and skills to explore more advanced territories.

# Exercises: Practicing Python Basics

In the quest to master Python Basics, let's embark on a journey through a series of exercises designed to sharpen your skills and deepen your understanding. These exercises are crafted to challenge, engage, and enhance your programming prowess, covering the fundamental concepts of Python syntax, variables, data types, operators, and input/output operations.

1. **Hello, Python**: Write a program that prints "Hello, Python!" to the console.
2. **Personalized Greeting**: Create a script that asks for the user's name and then prints a personalized greeting.
3. **Age Calculator**: Write a program that calculates and prints the user's age based on their birth year, which is input by the user.
4. **Basic Calculator**: Develop a simple calculator that takes two numbers as input and performs addition, subtraction, multiplication, and division.
5. **String Reverser**: Write a script that reverses a string input by the user.
6. **Temperature Converter**: Create a program that converts temperature from Fahrenheit to Celsius and vice versa.
7. **Odd or Even**: Develop a program that checks if a number entered by the user is odd or even.
8. **Word Count**: Write a script that counts the number of words in a sentence entered by the user.
9. **Simple Interest Calculator**: Create a program that calculates simple interest given principal, rate of interest, and time.
10. **Multiplication Table**: Write a program that takes a number and prints its multiplication table up to 10.
11. **BMI Calculator**: Develop a Body Mass Index (BMI) calculator that takes weight and height as inputs and calculates the BMI.
12. **List Sorter**: Write a script that takes a list of numbers from the user and sorts them in ascending order.

13. **Sum of Digits**: Create a program that calculates the sum of digits of a number entered by the user.

14. **Palindrome Checker**: Develop a script that checks if a word or phrase entered by the user is a palindrome.

15. **Count Vowels**: Write a program that counts the number of vowels in a string provided by the user.

16. **Leap Year Checker**: Create a script that determines whether a year entered by the user is a leap year or not.

17. **Number Guessing Game**: Write a simple number guessing game. The program generates a random number and the user has to guess it.

18. **Letter Repeater**: Develop a program that repeats each letter in a user-entered string twice.

19. **Area Calculator**: Create a script that calculates the area of a circle, a rectangle, and a triangle, based on user input.

20. **Fibonacci Series Generator**: Write a program that generates the Fibonacci series up to a number n provided by the user.

Each of these exercises is a step in your Python learning journey, crafted to build your confidence and competence in the language. They are meant to be both fun and challenging, pushing you to apply what you've learned in creative and practical ways. As you do these activities, you will understand more about how Python works and realize how simple and strong it is. This will make you even better at programming.

# Chapter 3: Control Flow in Python

**Introduction to Chapter 3: Control Flow in Python**

Welcome to the vibrant chapter of "Control Flow in Python," a journey into the realm where Python's logic and decision-making come to life. This chapter is akin to exploring the brain of Python, where you learn to guide its thoughts, decisions, and actions. Here, we delve into the essence of how Python programs make decisions and repeat actions, the crux of bringing dynamism and intelligence to your code. This exploration is not just about learning constructs; it's about weaving the fabric of logic into your programming tapestry.

We start by unraveling the mysteries of conditional statements – if, elif, and else. These are the fundamental tools for decision-making in Python, allowing your programs to react to different situations and conditions. Next, we dive into the world of loops with for and while, understanding how Python can efficiently repeat tasks and process sequences. These loops are the heartbeat of Python automation, pumping life into the static code. Further, we master the subtle arts of break and continue, the control statements that fine-tune the flow of your loops, giving you the precision to dictate exactly how and when your loops should operate.

# Implementing Conditional Statements (If, Elif, Else)

In the realm of Python programming, the ability to direct the flow of your program based on certain conditions is akin to being a conductor of an orchestra. Each musician plays their part, but it's the conductor who decides who plays and when. Similarly, conditional statements in Python - `if`, `elif`, and `else` - serve as the decision-makers of your program, directing the flow of execution based on specific conditions. Mastering these statements is like mastering the art of decision-making in your code, enabling your programs to react differently to different inputs or situations.

The `if` statement is a really important part of Python. It helps you make decisions and choose what actions to take. When you write an `if` statement, you're telling Python to do something only if a specific condition is true. It's like setting a criterion that decides whether a part of your program runs or not. For instance, an `if` statement can check if a user's input is a certain number, if a file exists in a directory, or if a list contains a particular item.

What happens when you need to check more than one thing at the same time? This is where the word "elif" comes in. It is short for the phrase "else if". An `elif` follows an `if` statement and checks another condition if the first one is false. You can have as many `elif` statements as you need, making it possible to check a series of conditions in sequence. Each `elif` is like an alternative path your program can take if the previous paths were not chosen.

Finally, the `else` statement catches anything which wasn't caught by the preceding `if` and `elif` statements. It doesn't require a condition; it's the path your program takes when all the other conditions are false. It's like the safety net of decision-making in Python, ensuring that your program can always do something, even if none of your specific conditions are met.

Using these conditional statements effectively requires understanding how to construct clear and meaningful conditions. In Python, conditions are like questions that can have two answers, "yes" or "no." These answers are called True and False, or Boolean expressions. These expressions can be as simple as comparing two values using comparison operators like `==`, `>`, `<`, `>=`, `<=`, `!=`, or they can be complex expressions involving logical operators like `and`, `or`, and `not`.

Let's consider a practical example to illustrate the use of conditional statements. Suppose you're writing a program that categorizes a user's input number into 'small', 'medium', or 'large'. You could use an `if` statement to check if the number is less than 10, an `elif` to check if it's less than 20, and an `else` to label all other numbers as 'large'. This simple program segment demonstrates the fundamental mechanism of control flow in Python - making decisions based on the conditions and executing code blocks accordingly.

Understanding control flow with `if`, `elif`, and `else` also involves recognizing how Python treats non-Boolean values in conditions. In Python, some things are considered true and some things are considered false. Things like words or numbers that are not zero are considered true. But things like nothingness or the number zero are considered false. This feature makes it easier for your computer to understand and follow instructions. It helps make the instructions shorter and easier to read.

However, with great power comes great responsibility. Writing conditional statements that are clear, concise, and correctly capture the logic you intend is crucial. Using really complicated or layered rules in your computer code can make it difficult for people to understand what the code is doing. Strive for simplicity and clarity in your conditions, breaking down complex logic into simpler parts if necessary.

In summary, conditional statements are the decision-making core of your Python programs. They help you make special programs that can change and react based on what is happening and the information they receive. As you progress in your Python journey, you'll find that `if`, `elif`, and `else` are your reliable tools for directing the flow of your program, making it behave differently under varying conditions. Like a skilled conductor leading an orchestra, you'll use these tools to create harmonious, responsive, and efficient Python programs.

# Introduction to Loops (For and While)

In the symphony of Python programming, loops play the role of the repeating rhythms and patterns, the persistent beats that drive the flow of the music. Just as a musician might repeat a series of notes to create a rhythm, loops in Python allow you to repeat a block of code multiple times, automating and simplifying processes that require repetition. This chapter introduces you to the two primary loop constructs in Python – the `for` loop and the `while` loop – each with its unique way of handling iteration.

The `for` loop in Python is like a skilled artist, precise and methodical. This is used to go through a group of things, like a list, and look at each one. It can be used for different types of groups, like numbers or words. The beauty of the `for` loop lies in its clarity and simplicity. It allows you to execute a block of code for each item in a sequence, making it ideal for tasks where you need to perform an action on or with each item of a collection. For instance, you might use a `for` loop to process each character in a string, each item in a list, or each key-value pair in a dictionary. The structure of a `for` loop is straightforward: you define the loop, specify the sequence to iterate over, and then write the code block you want to repeat.

While the `for` loop excels in situations where you know in advance how many times you need to iterate, the `while` loop shines in scenarios where you need to repeat an action until a certain condition is met. Think of the `while` loop as a storyteller who keeps the tale going as long as the audience is captivated. In Python, a `while` loop makes sure a certain piece of code keeps running over and over again as long as a certain condition is met. This type of loop is ideal for scenarios where the number of iterations isn't known beforehand, such as reading a file until the end is reached, or processing user input until a particular input is received.

However, the power of loops also comes with the risk of creating an infinite loop, where the loop never reaches an end. This is akin to a song that never stops, a rhythm that goes on endlessly without a pause. In Python programming, an infinite loop can occur if the terminating condition of the loop is never met. For instance, a `while` loop that checks for a condition that never becomes `False` will continue indefinitely, potentially causing your program to freeze or crash. It's essential, therefore, to design your loop conditions carefully and thoughtfully to ensure that they will eventually be met.

In Python, loops can also be used to go through a series of numbers. This is where the `range()` function comes into play, acting like a ruler that marks out the space for the loop to operate within. The `range()` function generates a sequence of numbers, which you can use in a `for` loop to execute a block of code a specific number of times. This functionality is particularly useful for tasks like running a loop a certain number of times, iterating through a sequence of numbers, or creating tables and lists of numbers.

Moreover, Python's loop structures can be nested – a `for` loop inside a `while` loop or vice versa. This nesting of loops is like weaving patterns within patterns, allowing for the creation of complex algorithms and operations. Nested loops are particularly useful in situations where you need to perform operations on multi-dimensional data structures, like lists within lists, or when you're dealing with problems that require multiple levels of iteration.

Loops can also be controlled using control statements like `break` and `continue`. The `break` statement is like a special button that you can press to quickly stop a loop from running. It makes the loop immediately stop and finish. It's a powerful tool that allows you to exit from a loop when a specific, often unexpected, condition is met. On the other hand, the `continue` statement is like a skip in a record; it halts the current iteration and jumps back to the start of the loop, beginning the next iteration. These control statements add a level of precision and flexibility to your loops, enabling you to handle a wide range of scenarios in your code.

To sum up, it's really important to know how to use loops in Python if you want to write programs that work well and get things done quickly. Loops provide a way to automate repetitive tasks, reduce the amount of code you need to write, and increase the readability and maintainability of your programs. As you get more comfortable with `for` and `while` loops, you'll find that they become indispensable tools in your Python programming toolkit, enabling you to tackle complex tasks with ease and elegance. Just like the repeating patterns in music that create rhythm and structure, loops in Python create a rhythm in your code, driving it forward and bringing it to life.

## Controlling Program Flow with Break and Continue

In the dynamic world of Python programming, controlling the flow of your programs is like being the director of a play. You can choose when a part of a story keeps going or when it suddenly stops. This power is wielded through two crucial Python statements: `break` and `continue`. Understanding and using these statements effectively is akin to mastering subtle narrative techniques in your programming script, enhancing both the functionality and readability of your code.

Let's embark on a journey to explore the `break` statement first. In the grand narrative of a Python loop, `break` acts as a decisive full stop. It's the command that immediately terminates the loop, regardless of its stage or condition. Imagine a loop as a circular track on which your code runs repeatedly. The `break` statement is like an emergency exit that can be used at any point to exit the loop instantly. This feature is especially useful in scenarios where you need to stop the loop when a particular condition is met, or when an unexpected situation arises that requires immediate exit from the loop.

For instance, consider a program designed to search for an item in a list. Without `break`, the loop would traverse the entire list, even if the item is found early on. By implementing a `break` statement that gets activated once the item is found, the program becomes more efficient, as it stops executing unnecessary iterations. This immediate exit strategy provided by `break` not only saves processing time but also makes your code more efficient and responsive.

Moving on to the `continue` statement, this command acts as a subtle skip or a jump in the loop's current iteration. When using Python, if you see the word "continue", it means to stop doing what you are currently doing and go back to the beginning to do it again. Unlike `break`, `continue` does not terminate the loop; it merely skips the part of the loop that follows it for the current iteration. This statement is akin to a director instructing an actor to skip a line and move to the next one.

The utility of `continue` becomes evident in situations where certain conditions within a loop require skipping, but not a full termination of the loop. For example, in a program processing a list of numbers, you might want to skip any negative numbers and only process the positive ones. By using a `continue` statement in a conditional check for negativity, the loop will bypass the negative number and proceed with the next iteration.

However, the power of `break` and `continue` comes with a responsibility. Overusing these statements can make your loops complex and harder to follow, much like a story with too many plot twists. It's really important to use them carefully, making sure they help make your code easier to understand and faster. A well-placed `break` or `continue` can transform a cumbersome loop into an elegant and logical flow of operations.

Moreover, understanding when and where to use `break` and `continue` is crucial. Their introduction into a loop changes the way the loop behaves, and thus changes the way your program executes. This change can be beneficial, like adding a shortcut to a long journey, or it can be disruptive, like a sudden detour in a well-planned route. As you gain experience, you'll develop a sense for when these statements can improve your program and when they might lead to confusion or errors.

In summary, `break` and `continue` are powerful tools in Python programming, giving you control over the flow of loops in your code. They allow you to manage the execution of loops with precision, either by terminating them early with `break` or skipping certain iterations with `continue`. Mastering their use is akin to mastering the art of directing in a play, where you control the pace, the scene transitions, and the flow of the narrative. As you continue your Python programming journey, these control flow statements will become integral tools in your toolkit, enabling you to write code that is not only efficient and effective but also clear and elegant.

**Conclusion of Chapter 3: Control Flow in Python**

As we conclude this enlightening chapter on Python's control flow, you now stand equipped with the essential tools to dictate the flow of logic in your programs. This chapter has been a journey through the decision-making pathways and repetitive constructs that form the backbone of Python programming. You've learned to utilize conditional statements to make complex decisions, unravel the power of loops for repetitive tasks, and precisely control these loops with break and continue.

Remember, mastering control flow is akin to mastering the art of storytelling in your programs. Just as a storyteller decides the plot's direction, you now have the power to guide your program's execution path, making it respond and adapt to varying scenarios. The conditional statements and loops are your narrative tools, helping you craft intricate and efficient programs. The use of break and `continue' adds nuance to your control flow, much like a storyteller uses pauses and emphasis to enhance a tale.

## Exercises: Building Control Structures

Embark on a journey through these carefully crafted exercises, designed to hone your skills in Python's control flow structures. Each challenge is a stepping stone to mastering the art of directing your program's logic and flow, a crucial skill in the repertoire of any aspiring Python programmer.

1. **Odd or Even Reporter**: Write a program that asks the user for a number and reports whether it's odd or even using an `if-else` structure.
2. **Temperature Advice**: Create a script that suggests wearing a jacket if the temperature input by the user is below 15 degrees Celsius, and wearing sunscreen above 25 degrees Celsius, using `elif`.
3. **Grading System**: Implement a program that assigns a letter grade (A, B, C, D, F) based on the numeric score entered, using multiple `if-elif-else` conditions.
4. **Positive Number Summation**: Use a `while` loop to sum all positive numbers entered by the user until they enter a negative number.
5. **Multiplication Quiz**: Write a program using a `for` loop that quizzes the user on multiplication tables, ranging from 1 to 10.
6. **Password Validator**: Create a script using a `while` loop that keeps asking the user for a password until a correct one is entered.
7. **Number Pyramid**: Use nested `for` loops to print out a pyramid of numbers, increasing in each row.

8. **Countdown Timer**: Implement a countdown timer that counts down from a user-entered number to zero using a `while` loop.

9. **FizzBuzz Challenge**: Write a FizzBuzz program that prints each number from 1 to 100 on a new line, using `for` loop and `if-elif-else`.

10. **Prime Number Identifier**: Create a script that checks whether a number entered by the user is a prime number using loops and conditional statements.

11. **Factorial Finder**: Use a `while` or `for` loop to find the factorial of a given number.

12. **Leap Year Checker**: Write a program that determines if a year entered by the user is a leap year.

13. **Number Guessing Game**: Implement a number guessing game where the user has to guess a secret number within a range, using `while` loop and `if-else`.

14. **Sequence Reverser**: Create a program that reverses a string or a number sequence using a loop.

15. **Simple Interest Calculator**: Using `if-else`, develop a script that applies different interest rates based on the principal amount entered by the user.

16. **Shopping List Handler**: Make a program using a loop that continually asks the user to enter the name of an item they want to add to their shopping list until they type "done".

17. **Age Group Categorizer**: Using `if-elif-else`, write a script that categorizes a person's age group (child, teen, adult, senior) based on age input.

18. **Odd Number Skipper**: Create a `for` loop that prints all numbers within a range, but skips odd numbers using the `continue` statement.

19. **Simple Calculator with Loop**: Design a calculator that continually asks the user for an operation and two numbers, performs the operation, and shows the result, until the user types "exit".

20. **Character Counter**: Write a program that counts the number of occurrences of a specific character in a string provided by the user, using a loop.

Each exercise is a brushstroke in the canvas of Python programming, allowing you to paint with the colors of logic and control. Through these exercises, you will not only practice coding but also develop a deep understanding of how and when to use Python's control structures effectively. As you work through these challenges, remember that each line of code is a step towards mastery, and each problem solved is a triumph in your programming journey.

# Chapter 4: Data Structures: Organizing Data Effectively

**Introduction to Chapter 4: Data Structures - Organizing Data Effectively**

Welcome to the enlightening chapter of "Data Structures: Organizing Data Effectively," a pivotal segment in your journey through Python programming. This chapter is akin to exploring a treasure trove, each data structure a gem with unique characteristics and uses. Data structures are the backbone of effective programming, providing the frameworks to store, organize, and manage data. They are the architects of your program's structure, defining the efficiency and logic of data handling.

In this chapter, we embark on a journey through various data structures that Python offers – each with its own story and strength. We start with lists, Python's versatile arrays that manage ordered data with elegance. Then, we explore the immutable nature of tuples, a data structure that guarantees the integrity of your stored data. Moving on, dictionaries are introduced as a powerful tool for key-value pairing, perfect for managing associative data. Finally, we delve into sets and their operations, where uniqueness and mathematical operations play a pivotal role.

Each section in this chapter is designed to deepen your understanding of how different data structures can be used to solve specific problems and optimize your code. By the end of this chapter, you will fully understand these basic ways of organizing data. You will also know which one to use when you are writing computer programs.

# Lists: Managing Ordered Data

In the world of Python programming, lists stand as a testament to the language's commitment to simplicity and functionality. As one delves into the chapter titled "Lists: Managing Ordered Data," it becomes clear that lists in Python are more than just a data structure. They are the backbone for organizing and manipulating ordered data, akin to a versatile toolbox, each tool crafted to handle data with precision and ease.

Think of a list in Python as a train. Each part of the train is like an element in the list. These elements can be of any data type - numbers, strings, even other lists - and they sit in the order you place them, waiting to be accessed, modified, or removed. The beauty of a Python list lies in its inherent ordered nature, allowing you to manage data in a way that is both intuitive and logical.

Making a list is easy. You just need to put the things you want on the list inside square brackets and separate them with commas. But this simplicity belies the power that lists hold. Since they are modifiable, you can alter their content without having to make a new list. This mutability makes them incredibly flexible, allowing you to adapt the contents of your list to the changing needs of your program.

Adding elements to a list can be done in various ways, each method akin to a different way of boarding the train. To attach an item to the end of the list, similar to adding the final carriage to a train, use the `append()` method. The `insert()` method allows you to add an element at a specific position, giving you the control to organize your data precisely. Alternatively, you can use the `extend()` method to add multiple elements at once, like attaching a whole new section to your train.

Removing elements from a list is equally versatile. The `remove()` method searches for the first occurrence of a given value and removes it, while the `pop()` method removes an element at a specified index. If no index is provided, `pop()` removes the last item, much like detaching the last carriage of a train. This flexibility in adding and removing elements makes lists an ideal choice for many programming scenarios, from simple data collection to complex data manipulation tasks.

Beyond adding and removing, lists in Python offer a myriad of methods for organizing and manipulating data. The `sort()` method rearranges the elements of the list in a specified order - ascending or descending. The `reverse()` method flips the order of the elements, allowing you to quickly invert your data sequence. These methods transform lists into dynamic tools for data management, adapting the structure of your data to your program's needs.

Python lists also support slicing, a powerful feature that lets you access a subset of the list. Slicing a list is like choosing a specific set of carriages from a train. You specify the start and end indices, and Python returns a new list containing only the elements in that range. This slicing capability is not just about accessing data; it's a way to create new lists from existing ones, to filter and process data efficiently and intuitively.

Furthermore, lists in Python are more than just containers for data. They are iterable, meaning you can loop through each element in the list, processing or examining it as you go. This iterability makes lists an ideal structure for tasks that require action on every element, from simple operations like printing all items to more complex processes like transforming each element based on certain criteria.

To sum up, lists in Python are an essential tool for organizing data. They provide a flexible, dynamic way to store, access, and manipulate data, making them an indispensable part of any Python programmer's toolkit. As you explore the capabilities of lists, you will find that they are not just a feature of the language; they are a cornerstone of Python programming, a reflection of the language's design philosophy that values simplicity, power, and flexibility. Whether you are a beginner just starting your programming journey or an experienced coder tackling complex problems, lists in Python offer the functionality and versatility you need to manage your data effectively.

## Tuples and Their Immutable Nature

In the diverse landscape of Python data structures, tuples stand out with their immutable nature, offering a dependable and unchangeable sequence of elements. This chapter, "Tuples and Their Immutable Nature," invites you to explore the unique characteristics and applications of tuples in Python, illuminating how their constancy can be a powerful tool in your programming arsenal.

Imagine a tuple as a time capsule, preserving a collection of items exactly as they were when the tuple was created. Once you define a tuple in Python, the elements within it cannot be altered, added to, or removed. This might seem like a limitation at first glance, but it is, in fact, a strategic feature that offers stability and integrity to your programs. Tuples are defined by enclosing their elements within parentheses, creating a simple yet effective container for your data.

Tuples provide multiple benefits due to their immutable nature. It first assures the integrity of the data. When you use a tuple, you have the assurance that its content will remain constant throughout the lifecycle of your program. For storing data that shouldn't be changed, such configuration values or fixed sets of data, tuples are a great option.

Moreover, tuples' immutability makes them inherently more memory-efficient compared to lists. Since the size and content of a tuple cannot change, Python can allocate a fixed amount of memory to store tuples, optimizing the resource utilization of your programs. This efficiency is really helpful in situations where using too much memory is a big problem, like in really big computer programs or tasks that involve a lot of information.

Tuples also play a significant role in Python's function arguments and return values. When functions return multiple values, Python packs them into a tuple, providing a compact and convenient way to pass around groups of values. This feature is especially useful in situations where you need to return a fixed set of related values from a function, such as coordinates from a geographical computation or multiple values from a complex calculation.

The unchangeable nature of tuples may appear to limit their functionality, but it opens the door to various creative applications. For example, tuples can be used as special codes in dictionaries because they can be easily turned into numbers. This ability to use tuples as dictionary keys enables the creation of complex data structures, such as multi-dimensional mappings, where each key is a tuple representing a point in a multi-dimensional space.

Tuples not only help you do things in your code, but they also make it easier to read and organize. When you use a tuple, it communicates to anyone reading your code that the set of values you are working with is meant to remain constant. This clarity can prevent misunderstandings and errors in collaborative coding environments or in large codebases where multiple developers work on the same project.

Furthermore, tuples support all the common sequence operations available in Python, like indexing, slicing, and membership testing. This compatibility allows you to manipulate and access the elements of a tuple in much the same way as you would with a list, but with the added guarantee of immutability. You can extract elements, check for the presence of an item, or slice a portion of the tuple for processing, all while maintaining the integrity of the original data.

Despite their immutable nature, tuples are not rigid or limited in their application. Tuples can hold different types of information, like numbers or words, and can even hold other tuples, lists, or dictionaries inside them. This versatility allows tuples to function as complex data structures, capable of representing sophisticated and multi-layered information in your programs.

Basically, tuples in Python are really cool and useful because they show how flexible and efficient the language is. They provide a stable, unchangeable structure for organizing data, ensuring integrity and efficiency in your programs. As you explore the world of Python tuples, you will discover how their immutable nature can be a valuable asset, simplifying the management of constant data, optimizing resource usage, and enhancing the clarity and structure of your code. Tuples may be unchangeable, but they are far from inflexible, offering a wide array of applications and benefits that make them an essential component of effective Python programming.

# Exploring Dictionaries for Key-Value Pairing

In the grand tapestry of Python's data structures, dictionaries emerge as a uniquely powerful and flexible tool. This chapter, "Exploring Dictionaries for Key-Value Pairing," is dedicated to unraveling the intricacies and applications of dictionaries in Python. Imagine walking into an archive room where every piece of information has a label and a corresponding record. Python dictionaries work in much the same way, storing data as key-value pairs, making data retrieval not only efficient but also intuitive.

In Python, dictionaries are like special containers that hold pairs of information. They are made up of curly braces, like this: {}. Inside the braces, the pairs of information are written with a key and a value, separated by commas. Each key-value pair is like a pair of friends. The key is the name of the friend and the value is all the information we know about that friend. The beauty of a dictionary lies in its directness – you use a key to access its corresponding value, much like using a word to look up its definition in a dictionary.

Python dictionaries are really cool because they can do a lot of different things and can be used in many different ways. Keys in dictionaries can be of almost any immutable data type, typically strings or numbers. Values, on the other hand, can be any Python object, be it a number, a string, a list, or even another dictionary. This flexibility allows for the construction of complex data structures that can represent real-world data more effectively.

Consider, for instance, the task of storing information about various articles in a library. Each article can have attributes like title, author, and publication year. A dictionary allows you to store all this information in a structured way, with each attribute as a key and its corresponding detail as the value. Such a structure not only organizes the data effectively but also provides fast and easy access to each attribute.

In Python, dictionaries can be changed. This means that you can add, remove, or change the things inside the dictionary after you make it. This mutability makes dictionaries incredibly dynamic – they can grow, shrink, and change as needed by your program. Adding a new piece of information to a dictionary is like writing down a new fact and connecting it to a key. Removing a piece of information from a dictionary is just like erasing it using a special word.

Python dictionaries also offer a variety of methods that enhance their functionality. The `get()` method, for example, provides a way to access the value for a key while offering a default value if the key is not found. Methods like `keys()`, `values()`, and `items()` give you access to the keys, values, or key-value pairs in the dictionary, respectively, facilitating iteration and data processing.

What truly sets dictionaries apart is their performance in terms of data retrieval. Accessing a value in a dictionary via its key is incredibly fast, irrespective of the size of the dictionary. This efficiency is due to the underlying implementation of dictionaries, which uses a data structure known as a hash table. This makes dictionaries an ideal choice for applications where speed and efficiency in data lookup are paramount.

Dictionaries find their utility in numerous real-world applications. They are extensively used in data processing, web development (especially in handling JSON data), configuration management, and more. In scenarios where data is naturally paired (like names and phone numbers, or countries and capitals), dictionaries provide an intuitive and efficient way of structuring and accessing this data.

In addition to their practical applications, dictionaries play a crucial role in Python's own internal workings. They are, for instance, the underlying structure for Python's objects, linking attribute names (keys) to their values. This fundamental use of dictionaries within Python itself is a testament to their versatility and efficiency.

In summary, dictionaries in Python are more than just a data structure; they are a paradigm for organizing and accessing data effectively. Their key-value pairing provides a straightforward and intuitive way of handling data, while their flexibility and performance make them suitable for a wide range of applications. As you delve deeper into the world of Python dictionaries, you'll find them to be an indispensable tool, simplifying complex data handling tasks and enhancing the efficiency of your programs. Exploring and mastering dictionaries will not only elevate your Python programming skills but also open doors to new possibilities in data management and application development.

## Sets and Their Operations

In the symphony of Python's data structures, sets emerge as a unique and potent composition. The chapter "Sets and Their Operations" is akin to exploring an uncharted island in the vast ocean of Python programming, where the treasure of simplicity and efficiency in handling unique elements awaits discovery. Sets in Python, akin to their mathematical counterparts, are collections of distinct, immutable elements, organized in an unordered way. They stand out in their ability to perform operations reminiscent of classical set theory, thereby opening a realm of possibilities for data manipulation and analysis.

Imagine a set as a pool of unique stars in the night sky, each shining distinctly, without repetition. In Python, a set is defined by elements enclosed in curly braces `{}`, or by using the `set()` constructor with an iterable. The essence of a set lies in its unordered nature and the uniqueness of its elements – no two elements in a set are identical. This characteristic makes sets particularly useful in scenarios where the individuality of elements is paramount and their order is inconsequential.

The true power of sets, however, is revealed through their operations. Sets in Python support a variety of operations that mirror those in mathematical set theory. These are different ways of comparing two sets. Union means combining all the objects from both sets. Intersection means finding the objects that are the same in both sets. Difference means finding the objects that are in one set but not in the other. Symmetric difference means finding the objects that are in only one of the sets, but not in both. Lastly, the symmetric difference operation finds elements in either of the sets but not in both, akin to finding stars that uniquely identify each of two constellations when compared with one another.

The operations of sets extend beyond these. Sets support methods that check for subsets and supersets, verifying whether all elements of one set are contained in another, or vice versa. This feature is akin to determining if one constellation is a part of another or encompasses another. In Python, these operations not only enhance the capability of sets but also make your code more efficient and expressive.

Moreover, sets in Python are mutable. You can add elements to a set using the `add()` method, or remove them using methods like `remove()` or `discard()`. The `update()` method allows the addition of multiple elements, broadening the horizon of your set. However, while sets themselves are mutable, the elements within must be immutable. This requirement ensures the integrity and uniqueness of elements within the set, maintaining its defining characteristic.

In practical applications, sets are invaluable in data processing tasks where duplicates are to be eliminated and unique elements are to be worked upon. For instance, in data analysis, sets can efficiently identify unique entries in a large dataset. In web development, sets can be used to process unique user IDs or session tokens. The usage of sets thus spans a wide range of scenarios, from simple data cleaning tasks to complex algorithmic solutions.

Sets also excel in scenarios requiring membership testing. Checking whether an element is part of a set is significantly faster with sets than with lists or tuples, especially as the size of the collection grows. This efficiency is due to the underlying implementation of sets, which uses a data structure known as a hash table. Such efficiency makes sets an ideal choice for large-scale data operations where performance is critical.

In summary, sets in Python are a blend of simplicity, efficiency, and mathematical elegance. They provide a unique way to store and manipulate data, ensuring the uniqueness of elements and offering a suite of operations that echo mathematical set theory. As you explore sets and their operations, you will uncover their potential to simplify and optimize your Python programs, making your journey in Python programming both exciting and fruitful. Sets may not always be the go-to data structure, but their specific characteristics make them an indispensable tool in certain programming scenarios, enhancing the effectiveness and efficiency of your solutions.

**Conclusion of Chapter 4: Data Structures - Organizing Data Effectively**

As we conclude the chapter on "Data Structures: Organizing Data Effectively," you stand at a vantage point, equipped with profound insights into Python's data structures. This chapter has taken you through a journey of lists, tuples, dictionaries, and sets – each structure providing unique ways to store and manipulate data. You've learned not just their syntax and operations, but also the nuances of when and how to use them effectively in your programs.

Remember, understanding data structures is more than a technical skill – it's about understanding how to organize and structure your data, making your programs more efficient and your algorithms more powerful. Lists offer flexibility, tuples provide immutability, dictionaries bring associative power, and sets introduce uniqueness and efficiency in operations.

As you progress in your Python journey, these data structures will be invaluable tools in your programming toolkit. They will help you tackle complex problems, optimize your code, and write programs that are not only functional but also elegant and efficient. The knowledge and skills you've gained in this chapter will be foundational as you delve into more advanced Python concepts and applications.

Embrace these structures as essential elements of Python programming. Experiment with them, apply them in various scenarios, and observe how they can transform the way you write and think about code. Data structures are the building blocks of effective programming, and with this knowledge, you are well on your way to becoming a proficient Python programmer.

# Exercises: Data Structures Manipulation

Embark on a journey of discovery and mastery through these carefully curated exercises, each designed to deepen your understanding and enhance your proficiency in Python's data structures. As you engage with these challenges, visualize them as a series of intricate puzzles, each unraveling the potential and application of lists, tuples, dictionaries, and sets in Python.

1. **List Reverser**: Write a program that reverses a list of numbers entered by the user.
2. **Tuple Pair Sum**: Create a script that finds pairs of numbers in a tuple that add up to a given sum.
3. **Dictionary Merger**: Write a function that merges two dictionaries into one, combining values for matching keys.
4. **Unique Set Elements**: Develop a program that takes two sets as input and prints a new set of elements unique to each set.
5. **Contact Book with Dictionaries**: Create a simple contact book using a dictionary where each contact's name is a key, and their phone number is the value.

6. **List to Tuple Converter**: Write a script that converts a list into a tuple.

7. **Dictionary Value Sorter**: Develop a program that sorts a dictionary based on its values in ascending order.

8. **Set Intersection Finder**: Create a script that finds the intersection of two sets provided by the user.

9. **Tuple Length Calculator**: Write a program that calculates the number of elements in a tuple.

10. **List Element Counter**: Develop a script that counts the frequency of each element in a list.

11. **Nested Dictionary Navigator**: Write a function that navigates through a nested dictionary and prints out all values.

12. **Set Symmetric Difference Explorer**: Create a program that finds the symmetric difference between two sets.

13. **Tuple Min-Max Finder**: Develop a script that finds the minimum and maximum values in a tuple.

14. **Dictionary Key-Value Swapper**: Write a program that swaps keys with values in a dictionary.

15. **List of Tuples Sorter**: Create a function that sorts a list of tuples based on the second element of each tuple.

16. **Unique Dictionary Value Extractor**: Develop a script that extracts all unique values from a dictionary.

17. **List Slice Printer**: Write a program that takes a list and indices as input and prints a slice of the list.

18. **Set Union Demonstrator**: Create a script that demonstrates the union of two sets.

19. **Tuple Concatenator**: Develop a program that concatenates two tuples into one.

20. **Dictionary Data Type Identifier**: Write a function that goes through each key-value pair in a dictionary and prints the data type of the value.

Each of these exercises is an opportunity to apply and solidify your understanding of Python's diverse data structures. They are designed not just to challenge but also to inspire you to explore the versatile ways in which lists, tuples, dictionaries, and sets can be manipulated and employed in Python programming. Through these exercises, you will gain a hands-on experience that complements the theoretical knowledge, shaping you into a proficient and inventive Python programmer.

# Chapter 5: Functions: Modularizing Your Code

## Introduction to Chapter 5: Functions - Modularizing Your Code

Welcome to the insightful chapter of "Functions: Modularizing Your Code," a journey into the heart of Python programming where structure meets creativity. In this chapter, we delve into the world of functions, the fundamental building blocks that provide structure and reusability to your code. Much like the chapters of a book that organize the story into coherent segments, functions in Python help you to segment your code into logical, manageable parts. This modular approach not only enhances readability and maintainability but also fosters code reuse and efficiency.

Here, we begin by exploring the art of defining functions and the crucial concept of scope, understanding how variables interact within and outside functions. We then navigate through the dynamics of parameters, arguments, and return values, which are the core mechanisms through which functions communicate and exchange data. The chapter further unfolds the elegance of lambda expressions, Python's way of creating anonymous functions for succinct and efficient coding. Each section in this chapter is designed to equip you with a deep understanding of these concepts, enabling you to write functions that not only perform tasks but also add clarity and elegance to your programming narrative.

# Defining Functions and Understanding Scope

In the grand narrative of Python programming, functions stand as the chapters of your code, each encapsulating a specific task or idea. The section "Defining Functions and Understanding Scope" is akin to learning the art of storytelling in coding. Here, you will delve into how to define functions – the fundamental units of reusable code in Python – and explore the concept of scope, which governs the visibility and accessibility of variables within these blocks of code.

Defining a function in Python is like drafting a blueprint; it's a plan for a specific operation that can be executed whenever needed. This is done by using a special word, the "def" word, followed by the name of the action or thing we want to do. And then we put the action or thing we want to do inside these round brackets. The structure of a function is a testament to Python's emphasis on readability and simplicity. Within its body, you write the series of statements that you wish to execute each time the function is called. This encapsulation not only makes your code more organized and readable but also reusable and efficient.

Imagine a function as a self-contained universe. When you define a function, you create a space where variables and logic exist independently of the rest of your code. This independence is crucial, as it allows functions to be modular and interchangeable without affecting the global flow of your program. However, this independence also introduces the concept of scope. In Python, scope means the area of the code where you can use a variable. There are two main kinds of scope: local and global. Local scope means that there are certain variables that can only be used inside a specific function and cannot be used outside of it. Global scope means that a variable is defined outside of any specific function and can be used anywhere in the code.

Understanding scope is essential, as it governs how data flows in and out of your functions. Variables defined in a function (local variables) are shielded from the rest of the program. This shielding ensures that operations within a function don't inadvertently affect the rest of your code. It's like having a conversation in a room; the discussion is contained within that space, not heard by those outside. On the flip side, global variables are like public announcements, accessible throughout your program.

The beauty of functions in Python lies not just in executing repetitive tasks but in structuring your program logically. Each function you define should ideally perform a single task or a closely related set of tasks. This singularity of purpose is key to effective function design. It's like writing a book where each chapter focuses on a specific part of the story, making it easier for the reader to follow the narrative.

However, defining a function is only part of the story. To bring a function to life, to make it contribute to your program's narrative, you need to call it. Calling a function is akin to summoning it into action. To use a function, you need to say its name and then put parentheses after it. Sometimes you also need to put something inside the parentheses called arguments, if the function needs them. This act of calling is where the function performs its task, whether it's processing data, making calculations, or any other operation you've defined within it.

In summary, learning to define functions and understand scope is like learning the grammar and vocabulary of a language. It empowers you to express complex ideas concisely and clearly. Functions bring structure, reusability, and efficiency to your code, while the concept of scope ensures that your code's architecture remains sound and logical. As you master these concepts, you will find yourself writing code that is not only functional but also elegant and efficient – code that tells a story in a clear, coherent, and captivating manner.

# Parameters, Arguments, and Return Values

In the realm of Python programming, the concepts of parameters, arguments, and return values in functions are akin to the characters, dialogues, and plots in a story. This section of "Parameters, Arguments, and Return Values" is not just about technical understanding; it's about grasping the essence of communication and interaction in the world of coding. Here, you dive into the intricacies of how functions receive, process, and return information, which is crucial for the creation of modular, reusable, and efficient code.

Let's begin with parameters and arguments, the cornerstones of function interaction. Imagine a function as a character in a play. The parameters are like the script lines given to the character, outlining what role they are to play. When you create a function, you get to choose what names you want to use for the information that the function needs. They are placeholders, a way of telling the function, "Expect to receive this information when you are called." Parameters set the stage for what kind of data the function will work with.

Arguments, on the other hand, are like the actual dialogues spoken by the character in the play. When you use a function, the things you give it are called arguments. They are like the important pieces of information that the function needs to do its job correctly. If parameters are the script, arguments are the performance, the actual delivery of lines. The subtle art of understanding and using parameters and arguments is crucial as it defines how information flows into and out of your functions, akin to the exchange of dialogues in a conversation.

When you call a function and pass arguments, Python matches each argument to its corresponding parameter in the order they are given. This process is much like filling in the blanks in a form. However, Python also offers flexibility in how you pass arguments. You can pass arguments by position, where their order matters, or by keyword, where you explicitly state which parameter each argument corresponds to. This flexibility allows for clearer and more readable code, especially in functions with many parameters.

Now, let's turn our attention to return values, the culmination of a function's operation. In a story, the plot builds up to a climax, the moment where the purpose of the story is realized. In a function, the return value serves a similar purpose. This is what happens when you use a function. It's like when you follow a recipe and get a delicious cake at the end. The outcome is the cake, which is the result of following the steps in the recipe. A function in Python uses the `return` statement to exit the function and hand back a value to the caller. This value can be any Python object – a number, a string, a list, even another function or none at all.

The beauty of return values lies in their versatility. They allow a function to communicate back to the caller, providing the results of its computations or actions. This makes functions not just isolated blocks of code but integral parts of a larger program, each contributing its piece to the puzzle. The ability to return values enables the creation of complex and interactive programs, where functions work together, passing data back and forth.

Moreover, understanding return values is crucial for effective function design. A well-designed function not only performs its intended task but also communicates its outcome clearly through its return value. This clarity is key to writing readable and maintainable code. It ensures that each function is a self-contained unit with a specific purpose and outcome, much like a chapter in a book that contributes to the overall story.

In summary, parameters, arguments, and return values are the fundamental components of function interaction in Python. They define how functions receive data, what they do with it, and how they communicate the results. Mastering these concepts is akin to mastering the art of conversation in programming, where functions speak to each other and to the larger program, exchanging information and building up to the final result. As you delve deeper into these concepts, you'll find your programming becoming more structured, modular, and efficient – a tapestry of functions, each playing its part in the grand narrative of your code.

# Anonymous Functions: Lambda Expressions

In the expansive universe of Python programming, lambda expressions stand as enigmatic and potent tools, akin to the wizards of a fantasy realm. This part of the chapter, "Anonymous Functions: Lambda Expressions," is dedicated to demystifying these powerful expressions, revealing how they imbue your code with conciseness and functionality. Lambda expressions in Python are anonymous functions, functions defined without a name, that can be created with a single line of code. They represent the idea of using less in Python, which helps you write neater and faster code.

The concept of lambda expressions can be likened to a haiku in poetry – short, succinct, yet capable of expressing profound ideas. In Python, a lambda function is like a small, quick way to create a function. You use the keyword "lambda" and then write what the function needs as input, followed by a colon. After that, you write the code that the function should do. This simplicity is what makes lambda expressions so powerful; they allow you to create functions in a concise manner, without the formal structure of a typical function defined with `def`.

Lambda expressions shine in scenarios where you need a small function for a short duration, and it doesn't make sense to formally define it. Imagine lambda expressions as tools for crafting quick solutions - they are perfect for when you need a function for one-time use, especially as arguments to higher-order functions that expect a function as a parameter. Functions like `map()`, `filter()`, and `sorted()` are common use cases where lambda expressions provide a neat and efficient way of passing functionality.

Imagine you have a list of pairs of things, like pairs of shoes. Now, imagine you want to organize these pairs of shoes based on the size of the second shoe in each pair. To do this, you would need to compare the sizes of all the second shoes and put them in order from smallest to largest. A lambda expression allows you to define a small function inline that is passed to `sorted()`, making the code more streamlined and readable. This application of lambda expressions for one-off, inline functions simplifies your code, reducing the need for multiple, single-use named functions that can clutter your codebase.

However, the power of lambda expressions extends beyond their brevity. They encourage a functional programming approach, where you start thinking of operations in terms of functions and transformations. Changing the way, you think about something can help you write code that is neater and easier to use. Lambda expressions can return any type of data, just like regular functions, making them incredibly versatile. They can return numbers, strings, lists, or even other functions, thus fitting seamlessly into various programming scenarios.

Understanding lambda expressions also involves grasping their scope. Being anonymous, lambda expressions have their own local namespace. They can access variables that are in scope at the point of definition, but they don't have an internal state that stores values between calls. This statelessness of lambda expressions is an essential characteristic that aligns with the principles of functional programming, emphasizing purity and lack of side effects.

Yet, the use of lambda expressions should be balanced with readability. While they offer a succinct way to define functions, overusing them or employing them in complex scenarios can make your code less accessible to others. The art of using lambda expressions effectively lies in recognizing when their brevity enhances clarity and when a regular function would be more appropriate.

Lambda expressions in Python are a special way to create short and unnamed functions. They are a helpful tool for writing code in a shorter and easier way. They are perfect for short-lived functions that are too small to deserve a name and are most effective when used in combination with functions that require other functions as arguments. As you explore the world of lambda expressions, you'll find that they add not just efficiency but also a touch of elegance to your Python code. Their mastery will not only expand your programming toolkit but also deepen your understanding of functional programming concepts, enhancing the overall quality and expressiveness of your code.

**Conclusion of Chapter 5: Functions - Modularizing Your Code**

As we conclude this chapter, you have journeyed through the intricate and fascinating world of Python functions. You've learned how to define functions, manage their scope, and communicate through parameters and return values. Moreover, the exploration of lambda expressions has opened up a realm of concise and powerful anonymous functions. This journey equips you with the tools to modularize your code effectively, turning complex tasks into simple, reusable components.

Remember, mastering functions is more than learning syntax; it's about embracing a modular approach to programming. Functions are the keystones in building robust, scalable, and maintainable code. They encapsulate logic and behavior, making your code more organized and your algorithms clearer. As you progress in your Python programming journey, these function-based modular blocks will be indispensable in tackling complex problems, enabling you to build applications that are not only functional but also elegant and efficient.

In this chapter, you will learn important things that will help you understand more difficult topics in Python later on. It's like building a strong base before going on to more challenging things. The art of using functions effectively will enhance your capability to think abstractly and solve problems programmatically. Embrace the power and flexibility that functions offer, and you will find yourself writing code that truly encapsulates the beauty of Python programming.

## Exercises: Designing and Using Functions

Embark on a journey to master the art of function creation and application in Python with these meticulously crafted exercises. Each challenge is designed not only to test your understanding but also to enhance your ability to think algorithmically and implement solutions using functions effectively.

1. **Simple Greeting Function**: Write a function that takes a name as an argument and prints a greeting message.
2. **Calculator Function**: Create a function that accepts two numbers and an operator (add, subtract, multiply, divide) and returns the result.
3. **Temperature Converter Function**: Write a function that converts temperatures from Celsius to Fahrenheit and vice versa.
4. **Area Calculator for Shapes**: Design a function that calculates and returns the area of various shapes (circle, rectangle, triangle) based on given parameters.
5. **Palindrome Checker Function**: Implement a function that checks if a given string is a palindrome.
6. **Email Validator Function**: Create a function that checks if an input string is a valid email address.
7. **Fibonacci Sequence Generator**: Write a function that takes a number n and returns the first n numbers of the Fibonacci sequence.

8. **Factorial Finder Function**: Develop a function that computes the factorial of a given number.
9. **Word Counter in Text**: Design a function that counts the number of occurrences of a specific word in a given string.
10. **Prime Number Validator**: Create a function that checks if a number is prime.
11. **List Filter Function**: Write a function that filters a list by removing elements less than a given value.
12. **Character Frequency Counter**: Implement a function that counts the frequency of each character in a string.
13. **Maximum Number Finder**: Design a function that finds and returns the maximum number in a list.
14. **Data Type Checker**: Create a function that returns the data type of a given object.
15. **String Reverser Function**: Write a function that reverses a string.
16. **Distance Calculator**: Implement a function that calculates the distance between two points in a 2D space.
17. **Age Group Categorizer**: Develop a function that categorizes a person's age group based on their age.
18. **Interest Calculator**: Create a function that calculates compound interest given principal, rate, and time.
19. **Leap Year Identifier**: Write a function that checks if a given year is a leap year.
20. **Password Strength Evaluator**: Design a function that evaluates the strength of a given password based on criteria like length, inclusion of numbers, and special characters.

These exercises are designed to stretch your ability to think in functions, encouraging you to write code that is not only effective but also elegant and modular. As you work through these challenges, remember that each function you create is a step towards becoming a more proficient and thoughtful Python programmer.

# Chapter 6: String Mastery in Python

**Introduction to Chapter 6: String Mastery in Python**

Welcome to "String Mastery in Python," a chapter that invites you on a journey through the intricate and fascinating world of Python strings. In this chapter, you will embark on an exploration that transcends basic string manipulation, delving into the realms of advanced techniques and the powerful art of pattern recognition. Strings in Python are not mere sequences of characters; they are the threads from which the fabric of data communication and processing is woven. This chapter is designed to elevate your understanding of these vital elements, transforming you from a novice to a maestro in the art of string manipulation.

We commence our journey with the basics of string operations and formatting, laying the foundation with essential techniques for manipulating textual data. Progressing further, we explore advanced string methods, unveiling the sophisticated tools Python offers for more complex text processing tasks. The crescendo of this exploration is the mastery of regular expressions, a potent tool for pattern searching that unlocks the ability to decipher and manipulate strings in ways you never thought possible. Each section of this chapter builds upon the last, creating a comprehensive guide to understanding and utilizing strings in Python to their fullest potential.

# Basic String Operations and Formatting

In the realm of Python programming, strings are like the clay in the hands of a potter – moldable, versatile, and fundamental to the art of coding. The section "Basic String Operations and Formatting" is a deep dive into the world of Python strings, exploring the myriad ways they can be manipulated and presented. This journey through strings is not just about learning syntax; it's an exploration of how to effectively communicate and present data in your programs.

Strings in Python are sequences of characters, and they come with a wealth of operations that allow you to manipulate these sequences in almost any way imaginable. The most basic of these operations include concatenation, slicing, and indexing – the fundamental tools for any string manipulation task. Concatenation is like string alchemy, where you combine strings to form new ones, using the `+` operator. This operation is not just about putting strings together; it's about creating new meanings, new messages, by joining words and phrases.

Indexing and slicing, on the other hand, are about precision – accessing specific parts of a string. Indexing is like finding a specific letter or symbol in a word by knowing where it is in the word, just like picking a book from a shelf by knowing where it is placed. The Slicing means you can take out a part of a word or sentence by choosing which letters or words you want, using a certain range of numbers. This is akin to cutting a piece from a cloth – carefully selecting the part you need for your purpose.

But the beauty of strings in Python lies not just in these basic operations, but in their formatting capabilities. Formatting strings is like dressing up your words – making them presentable, readable, and impactful. Python provides a variety of ways to format strings, from the older `%` formatting to the more modern `str.format()` method, and the very latest, f-strings. Each method has its unique syntax and advantages, but they all serve the same purpose – to embed values within a string in a neat and organized manner.

The `%` operator, reminiscent of the printf-style string formatting in C, allows you to inject values into a string using format specifiers. It's a bit archaic but still useful in certain situations. The `str.format()` method, introduced in Python 3, offers more flexibility and readability. It uses curly braces `{}` as placeholders within the string, which are then replaced by values passed to the `format()` method. This method is like a template, where you define a pattern and then fill in the blanks with actual data.

The newest addition to Python's formatting arsenal is f-strings, introduced in Python 3.6. They make string formatting more straightforward and readable. An f-string is a special kind of string that starts with the letter 'f' and has some special things inside curly braces. These expressions are evaluated at runtime and formatted using Python's formatting rules. F-strings are a game-changer in string formatting – they are intuitive, less verbose, and faster in terms of performance.

Beyond these operations and formatting methods, strings in Python come with a plethora of built-in methods for common tasks. These include methods for case conversion, like `upper()` and `lower()`, trimming whitespace using `strip()`, or finding substrings with `find()`. Each method is a tool in your toolkit, designed to handle specific string-related tasks efficiently and effectively.

In conclusion, mastering basic string operations and formatting in Python is about understanding how to manipulate and present textual data effectively. It's about knowing how to slice, dice, combine, and format strings to suit your needs, whether it's for data processing, user interaction, or generating output. As you become proficient in these fundamental string operations, you'll find that they form the bedrock of many Python programming tasks, from simple scripts to complex applications. Strings are the medium through which programs communicate with the outside world, and mastering them is crucial to becoming an effective Python programmer.

# Advanced String Methods

In the intricately woven tapestry of Python programming, advanced string methods are like the intricate stitches that add depth and texture to your code. Venturing beyond the basics, this section, "Advanced String Methods," takes you into the realm of sophisticated string manipulation. Here, you'll discover the powerful tools Python offers for processing strings, enabling you to handle textual data with a level of finesse and complexity that basic operations can't achieve.

Consider advanced string methods as the specialized tools of a master craftsman. They allow for more nuanced and intricate manipulation of text, much like how a sculptor uses finer tools to add detailed features to their work. These methods are crucial in scenarios where text data requires complex processing, such as data cleaning, preparation for machine learning tasks, or parsing structured text formats.

One way to break apart a sentence or word is by using the "split()" method. This method separates the sentence or word into smaller parts and puts them into a list. It does this by looking for a special character or symbol called a "delimiter" that tells it where to split the sentence or word. Imagine having a long sentence, and you wish to break it down into individual words. The `split()` method does this efficiently, splitting the string at every instance of a space, or any other delimiter you specify, and returning a list of words. This method is particularly useful in text analysis and natural language processing tasks, where breaking down text into components is a fundamental step.

Python also provides the `join()` method, which is somewhat of a counterpart to `split()`. This takes a bunch of words and puts them all together into one sentence, with a special word in between each one. This method is like a binding agent, bringing together disparate strings into a cohesive whole. It's invaluable when you need to construct strings dynamically, such as building a file path from different parts or creating a query string for a URL.

Another advanced tool in Python's string arsenal is the `replace()` method. It's like using a special tool to change some words in a sentence with different words. This method is akin to a precision eraser and pencil in one, removing specific substrings and filling in with new ones. It's particularly useful in data cleaning tasks, where you need to replace or remove erroneous data.

The `startswith()` and `endswith()` methods are like the sentinels of string processing. They allow you to check if a string starts or ends with a particular substring, respectively. These methods are particularly useful in file processing and web development, where such checks are frequently required, like verifying file extensions or URL structures.

Moreover, Python offers methods like `strip()`, `lstrip()`, and `rstrip()` for trimming whitespace from strings. These methods are essential in cleaning and preparing text data, ensuring that accidental leading or trailing spaces do not affect your data processing or comparisons.

Python's string formatting capabilities also extend into more advanced territories with the use of format specifiers in the `str.format()` method. This allows for detailed control over the formatting of values inserted into a string, such as specifying the number of decimal places for a float, formatting a number as a percentage, or padding a number with zeros.

The `find()` and `rfind()` methods are akin to detectives in the world of strings. They search for a substring within a string and return the position of its first occurrence (`find()`) or its last occurrence (`rfind()`). These methods are essential for tasks that require locating specific text within a larger string, such as parsing file contents or processing user input.

In simple words, learning advanced ways to work with words in Python gives us lots of cool things we can do with text. These methods provide the capability to handle complex string manipulation tasks with ease, making your code more efficient, readable, and powerful. As you gain proficiency in using these advanced methods, you'll find that they not only enhance your coding skills but also broaden your approach to solving problems in Python. They are the tools that allow you to sculpt and shape text data with precision, crafting solutions that are both elegant and effective.

## Regular Expressions for Pattern Searching

In the intricate world of Python string manipulation, regular expressions (regex) stand as the alchemists of text processing – transforming complex patterns into meaningful insights. The section "Regular Expressions for Pattern Searching" in Python's string mastery is akin to exploring a secret garden of text manipulation, where the most intricate and nuanced patterns can be discovered and utilized. Regular expressions are a powerful tool in Python, allowing you to perform sophisticated searches and manipulations on strings, going far beyond what basic string methods can achieve.

A regular expression is like a special code made up of letters and symbols that helps us find specific things when we search for them. It can be used to check if a string contains a specified search pattern, to replace parts of a string, or to split a string in various ways, depending on the pattern defined. The power of regular expressions lies in their ability to find complex patterns that would be difficult, if not impossible, to locate with standard string methods.

Imagine regular expressions as a magnifying glass that reveals the hidden structures within a string. They allow you to define rules that encapsulate the patterns you're interested in. For instance, if you're analyzing text data, you might use regular expressions to identify email addresses, phone numbers, or specific keywords, regardless of their position or the context in which they appear in the text.

Python handles regular expressions through the `re` module, which provides a set of functions that make it possible to search a string for a match, replace the matched text with some other string, or split the string in various ways. The most commonly used functions include `re.search()`, this is like a special tool that reads a sentence and tries to find certain words or patterns in it. It keeps going through the sentence until it finds a word or pattern that matches what it is looking for., `re.match()`, This looks for a match only at the start of the word or sentence, and `re.findall()`, this tool looks for specific patterns of letters in a group of words and returns a list of all the smaller groups of letters that match the pattern.

One of the key aspects of mastering regular expressions is learning the syntax that defines various patterns. This syntax includes special characters and sequences that have specific meanings in the context of a regex. An example is when you see a dot, it can stand for any letter or symbol except for going to a new line. The asterisk means that the letter or symbol before it can appear zero or more times. Square brackets `[ ]` are used to specify a set of characters you wish to match, and parentheses `( )` are used to group parts of the expression.

The real art of using regular expressions lies in how you combine these elements to form patterns. Imagine you have a special way of finding words that are exactly five letters long and start with the letter 'a' and end with the letter 's'. You can use the pattern "^a...s$" to do this. It's like a secret code that helps you find these specific words. Learning to craft these patterns is like learning a new language – one that speaks directly to the structure and form of text.

Regular expressions are very helpful for checking if data is correct. In web development, validators are like special tools that check if things like email addresses, phone numbers, and other things people type in are correct and make sense. In data analysis, they help clean and prepare text data, ensuring consistency and accuracy.

Having a lot of power means you can do a lot of things, but it also means you have to be careful and do things the right way. Regular expressions are very powerful, but they can also be tricky and difficult to understand. A poorly written regex can be cryptic and hard to maintain. Thus, it's crucial to not only understand how to write regular expressions but also to know when to use them. They are like a very helpful tool in your Python programming, but you should use them carefully and clearly.

In conclusion, regular expressions are an essential aspect of string mastery in Python, offering unparalleled capabilities in pattern searching and text manipulation. They open up a world of possibilities for analyzing and processing text, allowing you to unlock patterns and insights that would otherwise remain hidden. As you delve deeper into regular expressions, you'll discover they are not just a feature of Python but a powerful language in their own right, capable of speaking directly to the complex nature of text.

**Conclusion of Chapter 6: String Mastery in Python**

As we conclude our journey through "String Mastery in Python," you stand at the pinnacle of understanding, equipped with the knowledge and skills to masterfully manipulate and analyze strings in Python. This chapter has taken you through the foundational aspects of string operations, guided you through the intricacies of advanced methods, and unveiled the power of regular expressions for sophisticated pattern searching. Knowing how to use strings is very important in Python programming. It is a skill that you need to learn because it is used in many different things, like working with data and making websites.

Remember, the journey through string mastery is more than learning syntax and methods; it's about understanding how to effectively communicate and process textual data. The knowledge you've gained here empowers you to handle strings with precision and creativity, enabling you to write cleaner, more efficient, and more powerful Python code. As you move forward, these skills will prove invaluable, allowing you to tackle complex problems with confidence and elegance.

The art of string manipulation is a testament to Python's versatility and power. Embrace these skills, and you will find yourself capable of crafting solutions that are not just functional but also eloquent. May the mastery of Python strings not just be a skill you possess, but a tool you wield with expertise and finesse in your programming endeavors.

## Exercises: String Processing Challenges

Embark on a quest to refine your skills in string manipulation and pattern recognition with these thoughtfully crafted exercises. Each challenge is designed to push the boundaries of your understanding and application of Python's string handling capabilities. Let these exercises be your canvas, on which you paint with the codes and patterns of Python strings.

1. **Palindrome Validator**: Write a function that checks if a given string is a palindrome.
2. **Vowel Counter**: Create a script that counts the number of vowels in a provided string.
3. **Word Reverser**: Develop a program that reverses the order of words in a sentence.
4. **Acronym Builder**: Write a function that generates an acronym from a given sentence.
5. **Substrings of a Specific Length**: Create a script that extracts all substrings of a specified length from a given string.

6. **Character Replacement**: Develop a function that replaces each instance of a specified character in a string with another character.

7. **Alphabetical Order Checker**: Write a script that checks if the letters in a string appear in alphabetical order.

8. **First Non-Repeating Character Finder**: Create a program that finds the first non-repeating character in a string.

9. **String Compression**: Develop a method that performs basic string compression using counts of repeated characters.

10. **Password Complexity Checker**: Write a function that checks the complexity of a password based on specific criteria.

11. **Anagram Checker**: Create a script that checks if two strings are anagrams of each other.

12. **String Permutation Generator**: Develop a function that generates all permutations of a given string.

13. **HTML Tag Remover**: Write a program that strips HTML tags from a given string.

14. **Longest Word Finder**: Create a script that finds the longest word in a sentence.

15. **String-to-Integer Converter**: Develop a function that converts a numeric string into an integer without using built-in conversion methods.

16. **URL Encoder/Decoder**: Write a script that encodes and decodes a string to and from URL-encoded format.

17. **Letter Frequency Histogram**: Create a program that generates a histogram of letter frequencies in a given string.

18. **Common Prefix Finder**: Develop a function that finds the longest common prefix in an array of strings.

19. **Text File Analyzer**: Write a script that analyzes a text file and reports the frequency of each word.

20. **Email Extractor**: Create a program that extracts all email addresses from a given string using regular expressions.

These exercises are a blend of creativity and logic, designed to enhance your proficiency in Python string processing. They will guide you through various scenarios, from basic string operations to complex pattern matching, building a robust foundation in string manipulation and preparing you for advanced Python challenges.

# Chapter 7: File I/O: Reading and Writing Files

## Introduction to Chapter 7: File I/O - Reading and Writing Files

Welcome to the chapter "File I/O: Reading and Writing Files," an essential exploration into the world of data interaction in Python. This chapter is akin to learning the art of communication between your Python program and the vast universe of external data. File Input/Output (I/O) operations form the cornerstone of many programming tasks, from simple data logging to complex data processing and analysis. In this chapter, you are about to embark on a journey that will equip you with the fundamental skills to read from and write to files, a process that is as crucial as it is ubiquitous in the programming world.

We start by delving into the realm of opening and reading files, where you will learn how to access and extract information from various file formats. This is followed by an exploration of writing and appending to files, where you will discover how to record data and add to existing content effectively. The chapter progresses to cover handling different file formats, such as text, CSV, and JSON, each possessing unique characteristics and requiring specialized approaches for manipulation. As we journey through each section, you will gain comprehensive insights into the techniques and best practices for handling files in Python, laying a solid foundation for your programming endeavors.

# Opening and Reading Files

In the grand landscape of Python programming, the capability to interact with files is akin to unlocking a treasure trove of data. The section "Opening and Reading Files" in the chapter on File I/O (Input/Output) is a pivotal point, introducing you to the art of accessing and extracting information from files. This skill is not merely a technical necessity but an integral part of programming, allowing your code to interact with the vast world of stored data.

Opening and reading files in Python is like opening a book to reveal its stories. The process begins with the `open()` function, the key to accessing files. This function requires the name of the file you wish to open and a mode that determines the nature of the access you require. For reading files, the modes 'r' for read-only and 'rb' for binary read are commonly used. This step is akin to choosing the right key for a lock – selecting the correct mode is crucial for the operation you intend to perform.

Once the file is opened, Python treats it as an object, allowing you to interact with it using various methods. The most straightforward of these is the `read()` method. It takes all the words and sentences from the file and puts them together into one long sentence. Imagine it as casting a net that captures all the words in one sweep. However, this method can be problematic with large files, as it attempts to load the entire file into memory.

To handle larger files more efficiently, Python offers the `readline()` and `readlines()` methods. The `readline()` method is like a meticulous scribe, reading one line at a time, making it ideal for large files or when you need to process each line individually. In simple terms, `readlines()` takes all the lines from a file and puts them in a list. Each line of the file becomes a separate item in the list. This method is like gathering individual stories into a collection, allowing you to work with them as a whole or individually.

Another powerful feature of Python's file handling is the ability to iterate over a file object directly using a for loop. This approach is like walking through a garden and admiring each flower individually. It enables you to read and process each line as you go, making it memory-efficient and straightforward, especially useful for files with a large number of lines.

Python also offers context managers for handling files, using the `with` statement. This method is like having an assistant who automatically opens and closes the book for you. When you use a context manager in Python, it means that Python will help you with opening a file and closing it when you are finished using it. This not only makes the code cleaner and more readable but also ensures that the file is properly closed, even if an error occurs during processing.

Understanding file paths is another crucial aspect of file operations. In Python, when you want to open a file, you can tell the computer where to find the file by using either the exact location or by giving it a hint of where to look relative to where you are. An absolute path is like providing explicit directions to a location, while a relative path is like giving directions based on your current location. The decision between these options depends on what you need and how your project is set up.

To put it simply, being able to open and read files in Python is a really important skill for anyone who wants to be a good programmer. It opens the door to data processing, enabling your programs to interact with a multitude of data sources. Whether you are reading configuration files, processing text data, or importing data for analysis, the ability to read files efficiently and effectively is crucial. As you progress through these concepts, you will find that they form a core part of your Python programming toolkit, enabling you to build more dynamic, data-driven applications.

# Writing and Appending to Files

In the expansive narrative of Python programming, writing and appending to files is akin to crafting and continuing stories on a digital canvas. This section, "Writing and Appending to Files," unfolds the methodologies and nuances of these essential operations, empowering you to effectively record and enhance data within files. This skill is not merely about putting text into a file; it's an art of data preservation and augmentation, crucial for a multitude of applications from data logging to content creation.

Writing to a file in Python is similar to planting the seeds of information that will grow into a tree of knowledge. The `open()` function, just as in reading files, is your gateway. To write something in a file, you use the 'w' mode, which means write. When you open a file in this mode, Python prepares the file to receive new data. However, it's crucial to understand that if the file already exists, opening it in 'w' mode will erase the existing content and start afresh. It's like erasing a blackboard before writing new content.

In this mode, the `write()` method is used to inscribe data onto the file. You can think of the `write()` method as your pen, the string you pass to it as your ink. Each call to `write()` sends the provided string to the file, recording it exactly as provided. This method offers precision, allowing you to control exactly what and how data is written to the file.

Python also offers the 'a' mode for appending to files, which is akin to continuing an existing story without erasing the previous chapters. When a file is opened in append mode using Python, it adds new information without erasing what was already there. Instead, it positions the cursor at the end of the file, ready to add new content. This mode is particularly useful for tasks like logging, where new entries need to be added to existing data without disrupting what was already there.

Appending to a file uses the same `write()` method as writing. However, the context is different – you are adding to what exists, not creating from scratch. This difference is really important in situations where it's really important to make sure the information is correct and keeps going without any breaks. Imagine appending as adding new lines to a poem, each line enhancing the overall piece without altering the original verses.

Python also allows for more complex file write operations, such as writing multiple lines at once using `writelines()`. This method is a way to put a bunch of words on a piece of paper. It's like painting with a broader brush, allowing you to create more content in fewer strokes.

Moreover, the concept of file paths and modes remains as crucial here as in file reading. It's important to pick the right way and place to write your data so it goes where it should and in the right way. Additionally, using context managers with the `with` statement is equally important in writing operations. It ensures that your file is properly closed after writing, safeguarding against data loss or corruption.

In conclusion, the ability to write and append to files in Python is a powerful tool in your programming repertoire. It allows you to not only store data but also to build upon it, creating a dynamic and interactive data experience. Whether you're developing a software application, automating a data entry system, or simply storing information for future use, understanding how to write and append to files is crucial. As you navigate through these concepts and apply them, you will find yourself capable of handling a wide array of file-based operations, each adding a layer of depth and functionality to your Python programs.

# Handling Different File Formats (Text, CSV, JSON)

In the diverse ecosystem of Python programming, handling different file formats is akin to mastering multiple dialects of the same language. This segment, "Handling Different File Formats (Text, CSV, JSON)," delves into the intricacies of managing and manipulating various types of files – each with its unique structure and use cases. The ability to proficiently work with different file formats is a valuable skill in Python, akin to a key unlocking the doors to a wide range of data-driven applications.

The most fundamental of these formats is the plain text file. Text files in Python are easy to understand because they save information in a way that people can easily read and understand. Handling text files involves the basic file operations of reading and writing, as discussed earlier. The simplicity of text files makes them a universal tool for storing data. However, this simplicity comes with limitations, especially when it comes to structuring complex data.

Enter CSV (Comma-Separated Values) files, the next level in file format complexity. CSV files are really important when it comes to dealing with information and figuring things out, especially when we want to learn how things work and make predictions. They store tabular data, with each row representing a data record and each column a data field. Python handles CSV files through the `csv` module, which provides a reader and writer to interact with CSV files easily. The `csv.reader` and `csv.writer` objects are your primary tools for parsing and writing CSV files. They allow you to iterate over rows of the CSV and read or write data in a table-like format. This functionality is akin to an interpreter translating a foreign language into your native tongue, making CSV data easy to understand and manipulate.

The true power of Python's file handling capabilities shines when dealing with JSON (JavaScript Object Notation) files. JSON is a special way of organizing and sharing information on the internet. It is commonly used by websites and apps to talk to each other and share data. It is organized, not heavy, and simple for people to read and write. In Python, the `json` module is used to interact with JSON data. This module provides `json.load()` and `json.loads()` for reading JSON data, converting it into Python data structures like dictionaries and lists. Similarly, `json.dump()` and `json.dumps()` are used for writing Python data structures back to JSON format. Handling JSON files is like decoding a secret message – the JSON format neatly packages complex data, which Python can then unpack and convert into a usable form.

Working with these different file formats requires an understanding of the structure and syntax of each. Text files are like blank canvases, offering freedom but little guidance. CSV files introduce structure, organizing data in a tabular form, but still maintain simplicity. JSON files, however, are more sophisticated, capable of representing complex data structures with nested objects and arrays. This complexity makes JSON an incredibly powerful tool for web applications and data interchange.

In practical scenarios, choosing the right file format is critical. Text files are excellent for logs and simple data. CSV files are ideal for datasets that fit a tabular format, commonly used in data analysis tasks. JSON files are perfect for structured data, especially when dealing with web APIs or configurations.

In conclusion, mastering the handling of different file formats in Python significantly enhances your data manipulation capabilities. It allows you to interact with a variety of data sources, each formatted differently but equally important. Understanding these formats and their nuances enables you to choose the right tool for your data processing tasks, making your Python applications versatile and powerful. As you become proficient in working with these formats, you will find yourself capable of handling an array of data-driven tasks, from simple data logging to complex web data processing.

## Conclusion of Chapter 7: File I/O - Reading and Writing Files

As we conclude this journey through "File I/O: Reading and Writing Files," you now stand equipped with the fundamental tools and knowledge to adeptly handle file operations in Python. This chapter has taken you through the essential aspects of file I/O, from the basics of opening and reading files, to the more complex tasks of writing, appending, and handling various file formats. The skills you have acquired here are indispensable in the Python programming landscape, where data is an ever-present and vital component of virtually all applications.

Remember, the ability to interact with files is more than just a technical skill; it is a gateway to a world of data. Whether you are processing log files, analyzing datasets, or managing application configurations, the techniques covered in this chapter will empower you to handle these tasks with confidence and efficiency. As you move forward in your Python journey, these file I/O operations will continually serve as fundamental tools in your programming toolkit, enabling you to build more dynamic, data-driven applications. Embrace these skills, and you will find yourself capable of unlocking and harnessing the power of data in ways that elevate your programming projects to new heights.

## Exercises: File Handling Scenarios

Embark on a journey to master file handling in Python with these tailored exercises. Each challenge is designed to enhance your skills in managing and manipulating files, a crucial aspect of Python programming. These exercises will take you through various real-world scenarios, testing and expanding your abilities in file I/O operations.

1. **Text File Creator**: Write a Python script that creates a new text file and writes a given string to it.

2. **CSV Row Counter**: Develop a program that reads a CSV file and counts the number of rows.

3. **JSON Formatter**: Create a script to read a JSON file and pretty-print the contents.

4. **File Copier**: Write a function that copies the contents of one file to another.

5. **Unique Line Extractor**: Develop a program that extracts unique lines from a text file and writes them to a new file.

6. **File Extension Renamer**: Create a script that renames all files in a directory with a specific extension to another extension.

7. **Line-by-Line File Comparer**: Write a program that compares two text files line by line and reports differences.

8. **Word Frequency Counter**: Develop a tool to count the frequency of each word in a text file.

9. **Recursive File Finder**: Create a script that searches for files with a specific extension within a directory and its subdirectories.

10. **Image File Downloader**: Write a Python program that downloads images from a list of URLs and stores them in a specified directory.

11. **CSV Column Summarizer**: Develop a function that reads a CSV file and sums up the values of a specific column.

12. **File Encryption and Decryption**: Create a script that encrypts and decrypts text files using a simple cipher.

13. **Directory Size Calculator**: Write a program that calculates the total size of files in a directory.

14. **Batch File Renamer**: Develop a tool for batch renaming of files in a folder based on a specific pattern.

15. **HTML Content Extractor**: Create a script that extracts specific content (like paragraphs) from an HTML file.

16. **Log File Timestamp Extractor**: Write a program that extracts and prints timestamps from a log file.

17. **File Content Sorter**: Develop a script that sorts the content of a text file alphabetically and writes it back.

18. **Duplicate File Finder**: Create a tool that finds and lists duplicate files in a directory.

19. **File Permission Checker**: Write a script that checks and displays the permissions of a file.

20. **Markdown to HTML Converter**: Develop a program that converts Markdown files to HTML format.

These exercises are crafted to provide a hands-on experience in various aspects of file handling, from basic reading and writing operations to more complex tasks like file encryption and data extraction. They will not only bolster your understanding of file I/O in Python but also enhance your ability to apply this knowledge in practical, real-world situations.

# Chapter 8: Error Handling: Making Your Code Bulletproof

## Introduction to Chapter 8: Error Handling - Making Your Code Bulletproof

Welcome to "Error Handling: Making Your Code Bulletproof," a vital chapter in the saga of Python programming. This chapter is an odyssey into the realm of anticipatory coding, where you learn the art of foreseeing and managing the unexpected. Error handling in Python is not just about catching mistakes; it's about fortifying your code against potential failures and ensuring it performs reliably under diverse circumstances. This skill is indispensable, transforming good code into great, resilient software.

In this chapter, we begin by unraveling the basics of error and exception handling, laying the foundation for understanding Python's approach to dealing with the unforeseen. We then delve into the strategic use of try, except, and finally blocks, the primary constructs for managing exceptions in Python. These blocks are the pillars of robust error handling, allowing you to control the flow of your program and maintain its stability even when facing unexpected situations.

Progressing further, we explore the sophisticated territory of creating custom exceptions. This segment equips you with the ability to tailor error handling to the specific needs of your application, enhancing both the clarity and specificity of your error management strategies. As we navigate through these concepts, the chapter molds you into a programmer who not only writes code but also safeguards it, ensuring it stands resilient in the face of errors and exceptions.

# Basics of Error and Exception Handling

In the world of Python programming, error and exception handling is akin to building a safety net for your code. The section "Basics of Error and Exception Handling" in the chapter "Error Handling: Making Your Code Bulletproof" is a crucial part of this journey. It's about learning how to anticipate and gracefully manage potential problems that might occur during execution, ensuring your programs are robust, reliable, and user-friendly.

At the heart of error handling in Python is the fundamental understanding that errors are inevitable in any program. However, they should not lead to program crashes or unexpected behavior. Python, like many other modern programming languages, provides a comprehensive framework for handling these errors, known as exceptions. An exception is Python's way of saying, "Something unexpected happened, and I don't know how to deal with it." Understanding exceptions is the first step towards writing resilient code.

Exceptions in Python are more than just simple errors; they are objects that represent an error condition. When something goes wrong while a program is running, Python makes a special object called an exception to show what went wrong. If not properly handled, this object 'travels' back through the stack until it terminates the program and prints an error message, often much to the dismay of the user.

The beauty of Python lies in its approach to handling these exceptions. Instead of using error codes, which can be cryptic and hard to manage, Python uses a try-except block. The basic idea is simple: you try to execute your code, and if an exception occurs, you catch it and handle it in the except block. This approach is akin to having a plan B; if something goes wrong, you have a fallback to ensure your program continues to run smoothly or fails gracefully.

Python's try-except block is a powerful tool. Within the try block, you write code that you suspect might raise an exception. The except block then catches the exception and lets you handle it. Handling an exception could mean logging it, using fallback values, or even re-raising the exception with additional information. This process is not about making sure mistakes never happen; it's about handling them in a good way.

A key aspect of exception handling is knowing what exceptions to catch. Python has numerous built-in exceptions, like `IOError`, `ValueError`, `ZeroDivisionError`, and more. Each of these exceptions is meant for different error conditions. A well-written Python program should catch and handle the specific exceptions that it expects to encounter.

Moreover, Python allows handling multiple exceptions in a single except block or using multiple except blocks. This flexibility lets you react differently to different error conditions. It's like having multiple safety nets, each designed for a specific type of fall.

Python also provides the else clause, which is an often-overlooked part of exception handling. If nothing goes wrong in the try block, then the else clause will run. It's like saying, "If everything went well, do this." This separation of normal code flow from the error-handling code enhances the clarity and readability of your program.

In conclusion, mastering the basics of error and exception handling is essential in Python programming. It gives you things that help your code be stronger and easier for people to use. By understanding and implementing proper error handling, you not only improve the reliability of your programs but also enhance their maintainability and overall quality. As you venture into more advanced Python concepts, the principles of exception handling will continue to be a foundation for writing robust, professional-grade software.

# Using Try, Except, Finally Blocks

In the resilient world of Python programming, the use of try, except, and finally blocks forms the crux of creating bulletproof code. This segment, "Using Try, Except, Finally Blocks," delves into the strategic use of these constructs, which are instrumental in handling exceptions gracefully and ensuring your code's robustness and reliability. These blocks are not mere tools for error trapping; they represent a methodology for anticipating the unpredictable and safeguarding your code against the unforeseen.

The try block is like a protective shield that you put around a piece of code that might make something go wrong. It's akin to a testing ground where you cautiously execute operations that could potentially lead to errors. By enclosing this code within a try block, you are essentially saying, "I suspect this code may run into trouble, and I'm prepared to handle it if it does." This proactive approach is fundamental in Python, shifting the focus from error prevention to error management.

Following the try block, the except block is where you handle the exception. In essence, it's your safety net. When something unexpected happens in a certain part of the code, Python stops doing anything else in that part and goes to a different part that knows what to do in that situation. Here, you can specify different types of exceptions to catch and handle them accordingly. This selective catching is like having different responses prepared for different scenarios, allowing your code to respond appropriately to a variety of problems.

Python's flexibility in handling exceptions is showcased in its ability to have multiple except blocks. You can set up different responses for different exception types, making your error handling as granular as you need it to be. This is similar to having a team of experts, each specializing in resolving a specific type of problem.

The finally block is a critical component of this error-handling structure. It's like a set of instructions that always gets followed, even if something unexpected happens. The finally block is like a special place in a code where we can do important things like cleaning up and making sure everything is put away properly, like closing a book or giving back something, we borrowed. This means that important things are always done, no matter if something went wrong or not. This block can be likened to a responsible closure to operations, ensuring that everything is set right, irrespective of the outcome.

A common use case for try, except, and finally blocks is file handling. When dealing with file operations, numerous things can go wrong – files might not exist, they may be unreadable, or there could be issues in writing to them. By wrapping file operations in these blocks, you can catch and handle exceptions like `FileNotFoundError` or `IOError`, and ensure that files are closed properly using the finally block.

It's also worth noting that Python allows for an else clause in conjunction with these blocks. The else block is like a backup plan. It only happens if nothing goes wrong in the first part. This can be particularly useful for code that should run only if the try block was successful, thus keeping this code separate from the code in the try block, which enhances readability and maintainability.

In conclusion, the use of try, except, and finally blocks are a testament to Python's commitment to writing clean, robust, and error-resistant code. By understanding and utilizing these constructs, you can build applications that stand strong in the face of errors and behave predictably under unforeseen circumstances. As you become proficient in these error-handling techniques, you'll find them indispensable in crafting resilient and reliable Python applications, ready to withstand the rigors of real-world use.

# Creating Custom Exceptions

In the intricate craft of Python programming, the creation of custom exceptions is like forging unique tools to address specific problems. The section "Creating Custom Exceptions" in the chapter "Error Handling: Making Your Code Bulletproof" introduces a sophisticated aspect of Python's error handling capabilities. Custom exceptions are not just error messages; they are bespoke responses tailored to the unique needs of your application, providing clarity and control in how your program reacts to unforeseen situations.

Custom exceptions in Python are a powerful feature that allow programmers to define their own exception classes. These classes can encapsulate the specific error information that you want to pass along when something goes wrong in your program. By creating custom exceptions, you essentially create a new language for expressing the errors in your program, a language that is specific to the context of your application.

To make a special exception, you first make a new class that is like a copy of the class that already exists in Python called "Exception". This inheritance is what imbues your class with all the functionality of a standard Python exception, while also allowing you to add custom behavior and information. It's akin to creating a specialized tool based on a general design, modifying it to suit a specific purpose.

For instance, imagine you're building an application that interacts with a database. You might create custom exceptions like `DatabaseConnectionError` or `DataValidationError`. These exceptions can then be raised when specific issues related to the database operations occur. When you raise a `DatabaseConnectionError`, it's immediately clear that the issue lies with the database connectivity, as opposed to a generic `IOError` or `ValueError`.

The beauty of custom exceptions lies in their specificity and clarity. They enable you to convey a precise message about what went wrong, where it went wrong, and possibly suggest how to fix it. This specificity is immensely beneficial when debugging and maintaining your code, especially in larger applications where the source of an error might not be immediately apparent.

In addition to clarity, custom exceptions offer a way to encapsulate additional information and behavior. You can create special rules and information for your exception classes that can help you manage the problem better. For example, an exception class can have a method that logs the error to a file or database, or even sends an alert to the administrator.

Using custom exceptions effectively means thinking carefully about how and when to use them. It's important to ensure that they are used when truly necessary, and not as a replacement for standard exceptions. The aim is to make fixing mistakes in your program better, not more difficult. This requires a balance – creating custom exceptions for specific, significant error conditions in your application, while relying on Python's built-in exceptions for more general cases.

In conclusion, creating custom exceptions is an essential part of making your Python code bulletproof. It allows you to define how your program expresses and handles errors in a way that is both meaningful and context-specific. As you master this skill, you'll find that it not only improves the reliability of your applications but also makes them more maintainable and understandable. Custom exceptions are a testament to Python's flexibility, allowing you to tailor the language to the specific needs and nuances of your work.

**Conclusion of Chapter 8: Error Handling - Making Your Code Bulletproof**

As we conclude the chapter "Error Handling: Making Your Code Bulletproof," you have now journeyed through the critical aspects of crafting resilient Python applications. From understanding the basics of errors and exceptions to implementing try, except, and finally blocks, and creating custom exceptions, this chapter has equipped you with the tools and knowledge to write robust and reliable code. These skills are crucial in elevating your programming from merely functional to professionally sound and dependable.

Remember, effective error handling is a hallmark of a skilled programmer. It reflects a mindset that anticipates and plans for the unexpected, ensuring that your applications can gracefully handle unforeseen circumstances. The techniques and knowledge acquired in this chapter are not just best practices; they are essentials that define the quality and reliability of your code.

As you move forward in your Python programming journey, let the principles and strategies of error handling guide you. They will not only prevent your programs from failing unexpectedly but will also provide informative feedback when issues arise, making debugging and maintenance more manageable. The ability to handle errors adeptly is a key component of your programming arsenal, one that will distinguish your work in the vast world of software development.

## Exercises: Implementing Robust Error Handling

Embark on a journey to fortify your Python programming skills with these exercises focused on robust error handling. Each challenge is designed to deepen your understanding of managing unexpected situations in code, a crucial skill in crafting resilient and reliable applications. These exercises will guide you through various scenarios, reinforcing the principles and techniques of effective error management.

1. **Divide and Conquer**: Write a function that safely handles division, catching any division by zero errors.
2. **File Opener with Exceptions**: Create a script that opens a file and uses exception handling to catch and report errors if the file doesn't exist.
3. **Input Validator**: Develop a program that repeatedly asks for user input and uses exceptions to handle non-numeric inputs.
4. **List Index Safety**: Write a function that safely accesses an index in a list, catching index errors and returning a default value if the index is out of range.
5. **Custom Exception Creator**: Create a custom exception class called `OutOfRangeError` that is raised when a number is outside an accepted range.
6. **Temperature Converter with Exceptions**: Develop a temperature converter that handles exceptions for invalid temperature values.
7. **Safe List Average Calculator**: Write a program that calculates the average of list elements, handling TypeError for non-numeric types.
8. **Database Connection Simulator**: Simulate a database connection and use exception handling to manage connection errors.
9. **Recursive File Search with Error Handling**: Create a script that searches for files in a directory, handling potential filesystem errors.
10. **JSON Loader with Exception Handling**: Write a function that loads JSON data from a file and gracefully handles JSON decoding errors.
11. **URL Fetcher with Timeout Handling**: Develop a program that fetches content from a URL, handling exceptions for connection timeouts.
12. **Safe Square Root Calculator**: Implement a function that calculates the square root of a number, handling negative input values with exceptions.
13. **Memory-Conscious List Appender**: Write a program that appends items to a list and uses exception handling to deal with memory errors.
14. **Function Retry Mechanism**: Create a function that retries an operation if it raises an exception, giving up after a specified number of attempts.
15. **User Age Verifier**: Develop a script that verifies user age, using custom exceptions for age-related errors.

16. **Configuration File Reader**: Write a program that reads configuration settings from a file, using exceptions to handle missing file or settings.

17. **API Response Handler**: Create a function that processes API responses, using exceptions to handle unexpected status codes.

18. **Command-Line Argument Processor**: Develop a script that processes command-line arguments, using exceptions to handle invalid arguments.

19. **Network Request Retry on Failure**: Write a program that retries a network request if it fails, using exception handling to manage retry attempts.

20. **File Encoding Detector**: Create a script that detects the encoding of a file, handling exceptions if the encoding cannot be determined.

These exercises are crafted to not only challenge your understanding of error handling in Python but also to improve your ability to anticipate and mitigate potential issues in your code. As you work through these scenarios, you will gain practical experience in making your Python programs more robust and error-resistant.

# Chapter 9: Modules and Packages: Expanding Your Toolbox

## Introduction to Chapter 9: Modules and Packages - Expanding Your Toolbox

Welcome to "Modules and Packages: Expanding Your Toolbox," a pivotal chapter in the Python programming journey. This chapter is a gateway to enhancing your code's functionality and efficiency, akin to an artist discovering a broader palette of colors. Modules and packages in Python are fundamental components that provide a wealth of reusable code, enabling you to build more complex and efficient applications. By mastering these elements, you expand your coding toolbox significantly, making your programming endeavors both enjoyable and effective.

In this chapter, we embark on exploring the rich landscape of Python's built-in modules, diving into the depths of these pre-installed tools and how they can simplify various programming tasks. We then navigate the vast ocean of external packages, learning how to install and incorporate these additional resources into your projects, thereby extending Python's capabilities. The chapter further delves into the art of creating and organizing custom modules, empowering you to encapsulate and structure your code for maximum reusability and clarity.

As you journey through each section, you'll gain insights into the power of modular programming in Python. You'll learn not just how to use existing modules and packages, but also how to craft your own, tailoring your toolbox to your specific needs. This chapter is designed to equip you with the skills to effectively manage and utilize these critical components, making your Python projects more robust, scalable, and maintainable.

# Using Built-in Modules

In the rich landscape of Python programming, built-in modules represent a treasure trove of tools and functionalities waiting to be explored. The segment "Using Built-in Modules" in the chapter "Modules and Packages: Expanding Your Toolbox" is akin to unveiling a toolkit that has been expertly crafted to enhance and streamline your coding endeavors. Built-in modules in Python are the core components that come pre-installed with the Python interpreter, providing a plethora of functionalities that are essential for various programming tasks.

The essence of using built-in modules is rooted in Python's philosophy of 'batteries included', meaning Python aims to provide a rich standard library that caters to a wide array of programming needs. These modules are like the instruments in an orchestra, each playing a unique part to create a harmonious symphony. From handling dates and times in the `datetime` module to generating random numbers with `random`, and from performing mathematical operations using `math` to accessing the file system through `os`, Python's built-in modules cover a vast landscape of functionalities.

For instance, consider the `datetime` module, a cornerstone for managing and manipulating date and time in Python. This helps you control and understand dates and times in different ways, both easy and hard. Whether you're scheduling events, logging timestamps, or measuring durations, `datetime` equips you with the necessary tools, much like a Swiss Army knife for time-related operations.

Another pillar among Python's built-in modules is the `math` module. This module is akin to a mathematician's toolbox, offering a wide range of mathematical functions, from basic arithmetic operations like addition and multiplication to more complex functions like trigonometry, logarithms, and more. The `math` module is indispensable for any computation-heavy application, providing reliable and efficient mathematical functionalities.

The `random` module opens up the world of randomness and probability. It allows you to generate random numbers, shuffle sequences, and even choose random elements from a list. The applications of `random` are vast and varied, from developing games and simulations to random sampling in data analysis.

Additionally, the `os` and `sys` modules serve as gateways to the operating system, providing functions to interact with the system's hardware and environment. The `os` module lets you navigate, create, delete, and modify file directories and paths, while `sys` provides access to variables and functionalities that are tightly integrated with the Python interpreter.

Python's built-in modules also extend to more specialized domains. For example, the `json` module for handling JSON data, `re` for regular expressions, and `socket` for network connections. Each of these modules brings its unique capabilities, ensuring that Python remains versatile and adaptable to a range of programming scenarios.

Using these built-in modules is straightforward – they need to be imported into your Python scripts, and then their functions and classes become available for use. This is like picking the best tool from your toolbox for a specific task. The import statement is your way of telling Python, "I need these tools to complete my task."

To put it simply, it is really important to learn how to use the special tools that come with Python when you are learning how to write code. These modules are like the pieces of a puzzle that help us build strong, fast, and flexible applications. By leveraging the power and simplicity of these modules, you can significantly enhance the functionality and quality of your Python projects. As you delve deeper into Python's standard library, you will discover an ever-expanding universe of tools and functionalities, each designed to tackle specific problems and streamline your coding journey.

# Installing and Importing External Packages

In the dynamic world of Python programming, the ability to install and import external packages is akin to exploring an expansive library, where each book offers new knowledge and capabilities. The section "Installing and Importing External Packages" in the chapter "Modules and Packages: Expanding Your Toolbox" is a guide to accessing this vast repository of resources. External packages in Python are like specialized tools or add-ons that extend the functionality of your Python environment, allowing you to achieve more with less code and tap into a global community of developers.

The Python ecosystem is renowned for its rich selection of external packages. These packages range from those that handle data analysis and visualization, such as `pandas` and `matplotlib`, to web frameworks like `Django` and `Flask`, and to scientific computing libraries such as `NumPy` and `SciPy`. Each package serves a distinct purpose, offering a set of functionalities that can significantly streamline and enhance your coding projects.

To begin using an external package in Python, you first need to install it. This is where Python's package manager, `pip`, plays a pivotal role. `pip` is a powerful tool that handles the installation of packages from the Python Package Index (PyPI), a vast repository of Python libraries and modules. Installing a package with `pip` is like acquiring a new book for your library – it's a simple command that brings a wealth of knowledge to your fingertips.

Setting up something usually means you have to type a special instruction into your computer. To get a special tool called "requests" that helps with sending messages on the internet, you would use a special command called "pip install requests". This command instructs `pip` to download the `requests` package and its dependencies from PyPI and install them in your Python environment. This process is akin to picking a book from a vast bookstore and adding it to your personal collection.

Once a package is installed, it can be imported into your Python scripts using the `import` statement, similar to how built-in modules are imported. When you import a package, you make its functionalities available in your script. This is similar to opening a book to access its content. For instance, after installing `requests`, you can import it into your script with `import requests` and start using it to make HTTP requests.

Importing external packages also often involves working with namespaces. A namespace in Python is a unique environment where identifiers like variables, functions, and classes are mapped to objects. When you import a package, you essentially bring its namespace into your script. This can be done in various ways – importing the entire package, importing specific functions or classes, or even assigning an alias to the package to make it easier to reference.

The use of external packages also introduces the need for managing dependencies and package versions. As the things you make get more complicated, it becomes really important to keep track of the different versions of the things you need to use. Tools like `virtualenv` and `pipenv` help create isolated Python environments, ensuring that the right package versions are used, preventing version conflicts and maintaining consistency across development and production environments.

To put it simply, when you use Python, it's important to add extra tools and instructions from other sources. This is a basic and necessary part of programming in Python. It not only expands the range of functionalities available to you but also connects you to a global community of developers and their collective wisdom. By mastering the use of external packages, you can significantly enhance the capabilities of your Python projects, enabling you to tackle more complex problems with efficient, high-quality code. As you delve deeper into Python's rich ecosystem of packages, you will discover a world of possibilities and tools that can transform your programming experience.

# Organizing Your Code with Custom Modules

In the realm of Python programming, the creation and utilization of custom modules is akin to an architect designing and building unique structures, each tailored to specific functionalities. The section "Organizing Your Code with Custom Modules" in the chapter "Modules and Packages: Expanding Your Toolbox" delves into the art of structuring your Python projects more effectively. Custom modules in Python are not just about code organization; they represent a fundamental approach to making your code more modular, reusable, and maintainable.

The essence of a custom module is encapsulation. It involves bundling related code into a single unit, or module, which can then be imported and utilized in other parts of your program, or even in other projects. Think of a custom module as a specialized tool in your programming toolkit, designed by you and for you, to perform specific tasks or handle particular data types relevant to your project.

Making your own special tool in Python begins by creating functions, classes, or variables in a separate file that ends with .py. This file you made is like a special tool that you can use in your computer programs. You can use it by telling your program to "import" it, just like how you can use other tools that other people made. The beauty of custom modules lies in their simplicity and the powerful abstraction they offer. For instance, you might create a module for handling database operations, another for processing user inputs, and yet another for generating reports.

An essential aspect of custom modules is namespace management. When you create a module, you are essentially creating a separate namespace, which helps in avoiding name conflicts between your module and others, or between different modules within your project. This is similar to how different departments in a company operate; each has its own set of roles and responsibilities, yet they work together towards a common goal.

Custom modules also promote code reusability. Once you have created a part of a project that does a specific job, you can use it again in different parts of the project or in other projects without having to write it all over again. This not only helps you finish things faster but also makes sure everything you do is the same in all your projects. It's like creating a custom template that can be repeatedly used, ensuring uniformity and efficiency.

Moreover, organizing your code into modules makes it more readable and maintainable. When a project grows in size, having all your code in a single file becomes unmanageable. By segmenting your code into modules, each with a clear, defined purpose, you make your codebase more navigable and understandable. This modularity also makes it easier for others to read and contribute to your code, which is crucial in collaborative projects.

Another significant advantage of custom modules is the ease of testing and debugging. When your code is modular, you can test each module independently, which simplifies the process of identifying and fixing bugs. Imagine you have a puzzle with many pieces. Instead of trying to figure out the whole picture all at once, it's like solving the puzzle by putting one piece in at a time.

In conclusion, the practice of organizing your code with custom modules is a cornerstone of proficient Python programming. It enhances not only the structural integrity of your projects but also their scalability and adaptability. As you become adept at creating and using custom modules, you will find your code becoming more organized, efficient, and robust. Custom modules are a testament to the flexibility and power of Python, allowing you to tailor your programming environment to your specific needs and preferences.

## Conclusion of Chapter 9: Modules and Packages - Expanding Your Toolbox

As we conclude the chapter "Modules and Packages: Expanding Your Toolbox," you now stand equipped with an invaluable set of skills in Python programming. From understanding and utilizing built-in modules to installing and leveraging external packages, and from creating your own custom modules to organizing your code effectively, this chapter has broadened your programming horizons. These skills are essential in elevating your Python projects from simple scripts to sophisticated, well-structured applications.

Remember, the ability to effectively utilize modules and packages is what separates novice programmers from seasoned developers. It reflects a deep understanding of Python's capabilities and an ability to harness its full potential. The techniques and practices covered in this chapter are not just enhancements; they are fundamental to writing efficient, scalable, and maintainable Python code.

As you continue your programming journey, let the knowledge and experience gained from this chapter guide you. Embrace the power of modules and packages to avoid reinventing the wheel, to collaborate effectively with other developers, and to build applications that are robust and versatile. The world of Python modules and packages is vast and ever-evolving, and as you delve deeper, you'll discover an ever-growing toolbox that will continually empower your journey as a Python programmer.

# Exercises: Working with Modules and Packages

Embark on a series of engaging exercises designed to refine your skills in utilizing modules and packages in Python. Every challenge is a chance for you to practice and get better at this very important part of Python programming. These exercises are crafted to enhance your ability to integrate and manipulate various modules and packages, solidifying your proficiency in expanding your Python toolbox.

1. **Datetime Module Exploration**: Write a script using the `datetime` module to display the current date and time in two different formats.
2. **Math Module Application**: Create a program that calculates the area of a circle and the hypotenuse of a right triangle using the `math` module.
3. **OS Module Directory Navigation**: Write a script that uses the `os` module to list all files and directories in your current working directory.
4. **Random Module Game**: Develop a simple guessing game using the `random` module, where the computer picks a random number, and the user has to guess it.
5. **JSON Module Data Processing**: Write a script to read a JSON file, modify some values, and write it back to a new file using the `json` module.
6. **CSV Module File Handling**: Create a program that reads a CSV file using the `csv` module and prints each row along with its row number.
7. **Requests Module Web Scraper**: Use the `requests` module to download the contents of a web page and save it to a file.
8. **Pandas Module Data Analysis**: Write a script using the `pandas` module to read a CSV file, perform some basic data analysis, and output the results.
9. **Pillow Module Image Processor**: Develop a program that uses the `Pillow` module to open, resize, and save an image in a different format.
10. **Flask Module Mini Web Application**: Create a basic web application using the `Flask` module with a homepage and one subpage.

11. **Creating a Custom Module**: Develop your custom module with at least two functions and one class, then demonstrate how to import and use it in another Python script.

12. **Sys Module Argument Parser**: Write a script that uses the `sys` module to process command-line arguments for a file name and a file mode (read/write).

13. **NumPy Module Array Operations**: Use the `NumPy` module to create, manipulate, and perform calculations on a multi-dimensional array.

14. **BeautifulSoup Module for HTML Parsing**: Write a script that uses BeautifulSoup to parse an HTML file and extracts all the hyperlinks.

15. **Tkinter Module GUI Creation**: Develop a basic GUI application using the `Tkinter` module with buttons, labels, and text input fields.

16. **Pygame Module for Game Development**: Create a simple animation using the `Pygame` module.

17. **Scikit-learn Module for Machine Learning**: Use the `scikit-learn` module to implement a basic machine learning algorithm on a small dataset.

18. **Regular Expression Practice**: Write a script using the `re` module to find and replace all email addresses in a text with a placeholder email.

19. **Multiprocessing Module for Parallel Execution**: Demonstrate the use of the `multiprocessing` module to parallelize a simple task, such as calculating factorial numbers.

20. **Creating a Package**: Organize multiple custom modules into a package, demonstrate its installation, and show how to use it in a Python script.

These exercises are designed to offer practical experience in a wide range of applications, from basic file handling and data processing to web development and machine learning. As you work through these tasks, you will gain a comprehensive understanding of how to effectively harness modules and packages in Python, enhancing the sophistication and efficiency of your programming projects.

# Chapter 10: Diving into Object-Oriented Programming

**Introduction to Chapter 10: Diving into Object-Oriented Programming**

Welcome to "Diving into Object-Oriented Programming," a pivotal chapter that unfolds the sophisticated realm of OOP in Python. This chapter marks a transition from fundamental programming concepts to a more structured and powerful approach to coding. Object-Oriented Programming is not just a programming style; it's a paradigm that encapsulates real-world scenarios, transforming the way we think about and solve problems in programming.

In this chapter, we start learning about the basic parts of OOP - classes and objects. These are the building blocks that allow you to encapsulate and organize data in a way that mirrors real-life entities and relationships. We then delve into the concept of inheritance, a key feature that allows classes to extend and enhance each other, promoting code reuse and simplicity. Moving forward, we dissect the principles of encapsulation and abstraction, essential for safeguarding data and presenting a clear, concise interface to the outside world.

This journey through Object-Oriented Programming is designed to equip you with the tools and understanding necessary to structure your Python projects effectively. As you keep learning, you'll find out how using OOP principles can make your code stronger, easier to take care of, and able to handle bigger tasks. Each section is crafted to build upon the previous, weaving a comprehensive narrative that brings clarity and depth to your understanding of OOP in Python.

# Understanding Classes and Objects

Embarking on the journey of Object-Oriented Programming (OOP) in Python is akin to stepping into a new dimension of programming, one that offers a more structured and powerful approach to writing code. At the heart of OOP lies the concept of classes and objects, a fundamental paradigm shifts from traditional procedural programming. This section, "Understanding Classes and Objects," is designed to unravel the intricacies of these concepts, setting the stage for a deeper exploration of Object-Oriented Programming.

In the world of OOP, classes are like instructions for making special things called objects. These are like blueprints that tell us what things can have and what they can do. Like an architect's blueprint for a house, a class outlines the structure and capabilities of its objects without actually being one of the objects it describes. It's like a toy box that holds both toys and tools together.

Objects are things that are created based on a certain type or category called a class. If a class is like a plan for building something, then an object is like actually building that thing using the plan. Every object is like its own separate thing with its own qualities and things it can do, which are determined by its category or type. Creating an object from a class is called instantiation, and it is at this point that a class is given life in the form of an object.

To understand this better, consider a real-world example: a car. A car class would define attributes like color, brand, and engine type, and behaviors like accelerate and brake. Each car object created from this car class would have its own specific color, brand, and engine type and could perform the accelerate and brake behaviors.

In Python, when we want to create a new type of thing, like a toy or a pet, we use the word "class" to describe it. It's like giving it a name and telling the computer what it can do. We write the word "class" and then the name we want to give it, and then a colon. Within the class, methods (functions) and attributes (variables) are defined. These methods and attributes are what give the class its characteristics and behaviors. An attribute in a class could represent data like a name, an ID number, or any other characteristic, while a method in a class defines some action or behavior the class can perform.

Creating an object from a class is straightforward in Python. You simply call the class as if it were a function, and this call returns a new instance of the class, which is the object. Every object can have its own special values for the characteristics that are described in the group. This ability to create multiple, distinct objects from the same class is one of the key benefits of object-oriented programming.

One of the fundamental principles of OOP encapsulated in classes and objects is the concept of encapsulation. Encapsulation is like putting all the information and actions related to something together in one place. This means that encapsulation is like having a secret hiding place for an object. It keeps the object's inside secrets hidden from everyone else and only lets them see a special way to interact with it. It's like how a car hides its complex inner workings behind a simple interface of a steering wheel and pedals.

In simple terms, understanding classes and objects is really important when you're learning how to program in Python. It's like the foundation or building blocks of the whole thing! It represents a shift from thinking about code as a sequence of instructions to thinking about code as a collection of entities that interact with each other. This way of thinking not only makes code more manageable and understandable but also allows it to more accurately reflect the way we perceive and interact with the world around us. As you delve deeper into classes and objects, you begin to unlock the true potential of Python programming, opening doors to more efficient, effective, and scalable code.

# Inheritance: Extending Classes

In the world of Object-Oriented Programming (OOP) in Python, inheritance is a concept that stands out as a fundamental mechanism for extending and reusing code. It can be likened to the passing of knowledge and traits from a parent to a child. The section "Inheritance: Extending Classes" in the chapter "Diving into Object-Oriented Programming" is a journey into this powerful aspect of Python, where classes can inherit features from other classes, leading to efficient code organization and reuse.

In Python, inheritance means making new classes that are based on existing classes. It's like making a new type of toy using parts from an old toy. These new classes, known as derived or child classes, inherit attributes and methods from the existing classes, which are referred to as base or parent classes. This relationship not only represents a hierarchy but also a pathway for attributes and behaviors to be passed down. It's like a family tree where traits flow from ancestors to descendants, with each new generation inheriting features from the previous ones, while also introducing its own.

To understand inheritance in Python, consider an example of a base class named `Vehicle`, which represents general attributes and behaviors of a vehicle, such as `speed` and `move()`. From this base class, you can derive more specific types of vehicles like `Car` and `Motorcycle`, which inherit the properties of `Vehicle` but also have their own unique attributes and methods. This mechanism allows `Car` and `Motorcycle` to reuse code from `Vehicle`, making them more robust and reducing redundancy.

In Python, inheritance means creating a new class and telling it which class it is based on by putting the name of the base class in brackets. For instance, defining a `Car` class that inherits from the `Vehicle` class would look like `class Car(Vehicle):`. This simple notation belies the power of inheritance – it tells Python to bring in all the attributes and methods from the `Vehicle` class into the `Car` class.

Inheritance is like sharing toys with your friends. It helps us reuse and play with the same toys without having to buy or make new ones each time. In the same way, inheritance in coding allows us to reuse and use the same blocks of code again and again without having to write them from scratch each time. Instead of writing the same code again in the `Car` class that you have already written in the `Vehicle` class, you just inherit it. This not only saves time but also ensures that changes in the base class automatically reflect in derived classes, thereby maintaining consistency.

Inheritance also enhances code organization and readability. By organizing classes into hierarchies, you create a clear structure that models real-world relationships. This structure helps us understand and take care of the code better because it is organized in a way that is similar to how we naturally group things together.

Another important thing about inheritance is that you can change or replace certain actions in a method. Derived classes can provide specific implementations of methods from the base class. This is when a child class can have its own special way of doing something instead of using the way that the parent class does it. For instance, while both `Car` and `Motorcycle` will inherit the `move()` method from `Vehicle`, each can have a different implementation of `move()` that reflects their specific mode of movement.

In conclusion, inheritance is a cornerstone of object-oriented programming in Python that provides a powerful mechanism for extending and reusing code. It enables the creation of a hierarchical classification of classes that not only saves time and effort but also helps to create an organized, manageable, and scalable codebase. As you explore and implement inheritance in Python, you'll find that it opens up a world of possibilities in terms of code efficiency and sophistication, allowing you to build complex systems with less code and greater functionality.

# Encapsulation and Abstraction Concepts

In the intricate tapestry of Object-Oriented Programming (OOP), the concepts of encapsulation and abstraction stand as fundamental pillars, each playing a crucial role in crafting efficient and effective code. The segment "Encapsulation and Abstraction Concepts" in the chapter "Diving into Object-Oriented Programming" delves into these key principles, unraveling their significance in Python programming. These concepts are not mere technical terms; they represent a paradigm shift in how we approach program design, making our code not just functional but also intuitive and resilient.

Encapsulation in Python is akin to creating a protective barrier around the data and methods of an object. It is about bundling the data (attributes) and the code (methods) that manipulates the data into a single unit, or class, and then controlling access to that data. This is achieved through the use of private and public access modifiers. In Python, encapsulation is implemented using private variables and methods (usually denoted by a prefix underscore) that should not be accessed directly. This concept is similar to how people manage their personal information; they keep certain details private and only expose what is necessary.

Encapsulation is like a magic trick that makes it so we can't see how something works from the outside. It keeps all the secrets hidden! This helps keep the code safe from outside meddling and helps it work better by breaking it up into smaller pieces that are easier to handle. For instance, if you have a class `BankAccount`, encapsulation allows you to hide the account balance from direct access, exposing only methods like `deposit()` and `withdraw()` to interact with it. This ensures that the balance cannot be arbitrarily changed, protecting the integrity of the data.

Abstraction is like looking at the most important parts of something instead of all the small details. In Python, abstraction involves creating simple, user-friendly interfaces for your objects. This is achieved by exposing only relevant data and methods to the user, hiding the complex implementation details. Abstraction can be compared to the dashboard of a car. When you drive a car, you don't need to know all the complicated stuff about how the engine makes it go. All you need is the dashboard, where you can see and control the essential features like speed, fuel level, and temperature.

Abstraction in Python is implemented through the use of abstract classes and methods, often utilizing modules like `abc` (Abstract Base Classes). An abstract class is like a plan or a model that other classes can use to build themselves. This is a special class that tells other classes what methods they need to have, but it doesn't tell them exactly how to write those methods. It's like giving them a blueprint to follow, but they can choose how to build it.

When you use encapsulation and abstraction in your Python code, it becomes easier to organize, understand, and protect. Encapsulation ensures that the data is safe and exposed only through controlled methods, while abstraction provides a clear and simple interface for interacting with objects. This combination not only improves the quality of the code but also enhances the user experience, making complex systems easier to understand and work with.

In conclusion, understanding and implementing encapsulation and abstraction are key to proficient Python programming. These concepts empower you to build applications that are not only efficient and secure but also user-friendly and adaptable. As you delve deeper into object-oriented programming, the mastery of encapsulation and abstraction will enable you to create complex applications with elegant and intuitive interfaces, making your code not just a set of instructions but a work of art.

**Conclusion of Chapter 10: Diving into Object-Oriented Programming**

As we conclude "Diving into Object-Oriented Programming," you now stand on the threshold of advanced Python programming. This chapter has guided you through the core principles of OOP, a methodology that underpins modern software development. By embracing classes and objects, inheritance, encapsulation, and abstraction, you've gained insights into structuring your code in ways that enhance its functionality, maintainability, and scalability.

Remember, the journey into OOP is more than learning a new set of tools; it's about adopting a new perspective on programming. The object-oriented approach aligns closely with how we perceive the real world, allowing us to model complex systems more naturally and intuitively. This chapter has laid the groundwork for you to think and code like an experienced object-oriented programmer, enabling you to tackle complex programming challenges with greater ease and sophistication.

As you continue to hone your skills, let the concepts and practices of OOP guide your programming decisions. The ability to effectively implement these principles will significantly impact the quality of your software projects, making them not only robust and efficient but also adaptable to evolving requirements. Embrace the full potential of Object-Oriented Programming, and you'll unlock new horizons in your Python programming journey, building software that stands the test of time.

# Exercises: Object-Oriented Design and Implementation

In the realm of Object-Oriented Programming, practical exercises play a crucial role in solidifying understanding and enhancing skill. The section "Exercises: Object-Oriented Design and Implementation" in the chapter "Diving into Object-Oriented Programming" presents a series of challenges designed to deepen your grasp of OOP concepts in Python. These exercises are crafted to encourage creative thinking and problem-solving within the framework of OOP principles.

1. **Basic Class Creation**: Define a class `Book` with attributes like title, author, and publication year. Include a method to display book information.
2. **Inheritance Implementation**: Create a `Vehicle` class and extend it with specific vehicle types like `Car` and `Truck`, adding unique attributes to each.
3. **Encapsulation Practice**: Design a `BankAccount` class where the balance is kept private. Implement public methods for depositing, withdrawing, and viewing the balance.
4. **Abstract Class Usage**: Define an abstract class `Shape` with an abstract method for area calculation. Create subclasses like `Circle` and `Rectangle` implementing the area method.
5. **Polymorphism Demonstration**: Create a function that takes different shapes (instances of `Shape` subclasses) and prints their area, demonstrating polymorphism.
6. **Complex Inheritance Structure**: Design a class hierarchy for a university system including classes like `Person`, `Student`, `Staff`, and `Instructor`.
7. **Method Overriding**: Create a class `Bird` with a method `fly()`. Extend it into classes like `Sparrow` and `Ostrich`, where `fly` behaves differently.
8. **Multi-level Inheritance**: Develop a three-level inheritance structure starting with a `Vehicle`, extending to `ElectricVehicle`, and then to `ElectricCar`.
9. **Composition over Inheritance**: Implement a class `Engine`, and use it as a component of a `Car` class instead of using inheritance.
10. **Operator Overloading**: Overload operators in a class `Fraction` to support addition, subtraction, and comparison of fraction objects.

11. **Property Decorators**: Use property decorators in a class `Temperature` to get and set temperature in Celsius, while internally storing it in Fahrenheit.

12. **Private Methods**: In a class `Calculator`, implement private methods for internal calculations and public methods to expose functionalities like add and subtract.

13. **Static and Class Methods**: Create a class `DateParser` with static and class methods to handle different formats of date strings.

14. **Class Aggregation**: Design two classes, `Author` and `Book`, where each book can have one or more authors, demonstrating the concept of aggregation.

15. **Custom Iterator Class**: Implement a custom iterator in a class `Countdown` that counts down from a given number.

16. **Singleton Pattern**: Create a singleton class `DatabaseConnector` to ensure only one instance of the connector exists in the program.

17. **Factory Method Implementation**: Use a factory method in a class `Animal` to create and return objects of different animal types based on input.

18. **Mixins Usage**: Create mixin classes to add additional functionalities like JSONSerializable and XMLSerializable to other classes.

19. **Multiple Inheritance**: Design a class `FlyingCar` that inherits from both `Car` and `Airplane` classes, managing the complexities of multiple inheritance.

20. **Dependency Injection**: Implement dependency injection in a class `BookReader` where the method of reading (e.g., from file, API) is injected into the class.

These exercises are designed to challenge and refine your understanding of OOP in Python, covering a range of topics from basic class structures to more complex design patterns. As you work through these exercises, you will gain a deeper appreciation and proficiency in implementing object-oriented solutions to programming problems.

# Chapter 11: Advanced Topics in Python

## Introduction to Chapter 11: Advanced Topics in Python

Welcome to "Advanced Topics in Python," a chapter designed to take your Python skills beyond the ordinary and into the realm of the extraordinary. This chapter serves as a bridge to the more sophisticated aspects of Python programming, introducing concepts that will empower you to write cleaner, more efficient, and more powerful code. Python, known for its simplicity and readability, also offers a depth of functionality for those willing to delve deeper, and this chapter is your guide into these deeper waters.

In this chapter, we explore the elegant and powerful feature of decorators, which allow you to enhance and modify the behavior of your functions dynamically. We then delve into the world of iterators and generators, tools that offer a more memory-efficient way of iterating over data. Comprehensions, with their concise and expressive syntax for creating new sequences, are also covered, showcasing their efficiency in data processing. Lastly, we explore context managers, an exceptional feature of Python that simplifies resource management, ensuring that resources like files and network connections are handled safely and efficiently.

Each section of this chapter is crafted to not only introduce you to these advanced concepts but also to demonstrate their practical applications. As you progress, you will discover new ways to solve problems, optimize your code, and harness the full potential of Python programming.

# Decorators: Enhancing Functionality

In the advanced landscape of Python programming, decorators stand as a fascinating and powerful feature, offering a dynamic way to modify and enhance the functionality of code. The segment "Decorators: Enhancing Functionality" in the chapter "Advanced Topics in Python" is dedicated to unraveling the intricacies and potential of decorators. These are not just mere tools for code embellishment; they represent a profound mechanism for extending functionality in a clean, readable, and efficient manner.

A decorator in Python is like adding extra powers to a superhero. It is a special function that takes another function as its friend and gives it some extra abilities, without changing the original function. This concept is akin to adding a new layer of paint to a room; the underlying structure remains the same, but its appearance and character are transformed. Decorators are like special tools that can change how a function or method works in a way that is easy to understand and change.

The essence of understanding decorators lies in grasping higher-order functions in Python. A higher-order function is like a special kind of function that can either use another function or give you a new function. Decorators leverage this concept by being a higher-order function that wraps another function, enhancing or changing its behavior.

To make something look more special, you use a special tool called a decorator. You start by making a special type of function that can take another function as a special ingredient. Within this outer function, another function is defined, often called the wrapper. This wrapper function is where the additional functionality is implemented. After executing this additional functionality, the wrapper calls the original function, or it might choose not to call it, depending on the intended behavior. At the end, the main function gives back the special function that was made inside it.

Imagine you have a special tool that can measure how long it takes for someone to finish a task. In this case, the task is a special kind of action called a function. So, you can use the tool to see how much time it takes for the function to finish its work. You could create a decorator that starts a timer before calling the function and stops the timer after the function completes, thereby calculating the total execution time. This enhancement is done without altering the original function's code.

Using decorators in Python is elegantly simple, thanks to the '@' syntax, also known as syntactic sugar. You apply a decorator to a function by placing the decorator's name preceded by an '@' above the function's definition. The '@' symbol in Python is a way to tell the computer to use a special tool on a specific function." It's an intuitive and visually clear way of attaching additional functionality to existing code.

Decorators are like building blocks that you can put on top of each other to make something even more powerful. You can add different special things to a toy, like stickers or paint, to make it more fun and interesting. With each special thing you add, the toy becomes even cooler and more unique. This stacking is done in a way that the decorator closest to the function runs first and the furthest runs last. It's a composition of functionalities, each layer building upon the previous one.

Decorators also play a significant role in web development frameworks like Flask and Django, particularly in handling routes and views. They are used to connect URLs to Python functions, making it easy to define routes in a web application.

In conclusion, decorators are a quintessential aspect of advanced Python programming. They help make functions do more things without changing how they work inside. Learning and using decorators can help you write better and neater code in Python. They encourage a modular approach to programming, where enhancements and changes can be made in a decoupled manner. As you explore the world of decorators, you will uncover a new level of programming prowess, unlocking the potential to solve problems in more creative and effective ways.

## Iterators and Generators

In the advanced expedition of Python programming, iterators and generators emerge as powerful concepts that significantly enhance the efficiency and performance of your code. The section "Iterators and Generators" in the chapter "Advanced Topics in Python" delves into these sophisticated constructs, shedding light on their mechanisms and practical applications. These are not mere programming gimmicks; they are fundamental tools that enable efficient data processing and manipulation, especially in scenarios involving large datasets.

An iterator in Python is like a tool that helps us look at each item in a group, like a list or a special group we made ourselves. Iterators are like magic wands that let you see and use one thing at a time from a big group of things, without having to see or use all the things at once. This feature is really helpful when working with a lot of information, because it uses less computer memory and makes things work faster.

To understand iterators, one must first understand the concept of iterables. An iterable is like a box of toys that you can play with one at a time. It allows you to go through each toy in a loop and have fun with it! Lists, tuples, dictionaries, and sets are all things that we can use to store and organize information. They are called "iterables" because we can go through each item in them one by one. An iterator is like a special tool that helps us go through a group of things one by one. It can remember where we left off and helps us keep track of what we have already looked at.

In Python, iterators are implemented using two special methods, `__iter__()` and `__next__()`. The `__iter__()` method, which is called when an iterator is initialized, returns the iterator object itself. The `__next__()` method gives us the next thing in the group. When you finish looking at all the things, the program will raise a special message called "StopIteration" to tell you that you are done looking at the things.

Generators are like a special tool that can help us make things that go in order. They are simple to use and can do really cool things! These functions are written in a special way. They look like normal functions, but instead of returning all the data at once, they return a little bit of data at a time using the keyword "yield". When we use a generator function, it doesn't start doing everything right away. Instead, it gives us a special object that we can use to do things step by step. This object can then be used in a for loop, which will execute the generator's code up to the first `yield` statement, return the yielded value, and pause the function's state until the next value is requested.

The true power of generators is their ability to generate values on the fly, which means they don't have the memory constraints of storing large datasets. For instance, a generator can be used to read lines from a large file or generate an infinite sequence of numbers. This on-the-fly data generation makes generators an excellent choice for working with data streams or large datasets where it's impractical or impossible to hold all the data in memory at once.

Generators also simplify the code. Instead of writing classes with `__iter__()` and `__next__()` methods, you can simply write a function with yield statements. This makes the code easier to read and understand, easier to keep up-to-date, and makes it clearer and more effective.

In conclusion, iterators and generators are indispensable tools in the arsenal of a Python programmer, particularly when dealing with data-intensive tasks. They offer a memory-efficient and elegant way to iterate over data, load it lazily, and handle large datasets with ease. As you explore these concepts, you'll discover a new realm of possibilities for data processing and manipulation, allowing you to write more efficient, scalable, and cleaner Python code. These tools exemplify the elegance and power of Python, enabling you to tackle complex data-related challenges with simplicity and grace.

## Comprehensions for Efficient Data Processing

In the panorama of Python's advanced topics, comprehensions stand out as a sleek and efficient tool for data processing. The section "Comprehensions for Efficient Data Processing" in the chapter "Advanced Topics in Python" explores this elegant Python feature that allows for creating new sequences in a clear and concise way. Comprehensions are not just syntactic sugar; they are a paradigm that epitomizes Python's ethos of writing readable, efficient, and expressive code.

Python comprehensions come in various forms: list comprehensions, dictionary comprehensions, set comprehensions, and, in some aspects, generator expressions. Each serves a unique purpose and adds a layer of efficiency and clarity to data manipulation. They transform what would typically be multi-line loops and conditional statements into single-line, readable, and concise expressions.

A list comprehension in Python provides a compact way of creating lists. This thing has brackets with something inside called an expression. After the expression, there is a special word called "for" and then there can be more special words called "for" or "if" but you don't have to have any of them if you don't want to. You can use different things, like toys or food, to make a list. The result is a new list that is made by looking at a certain rule and checking if something is true or not. This code takes the numbers from 0 to 9 and makes a new list with their squares. So, instead of just having the numbers themselves, we have their squares in the new list.

Dictionary comprehensions are like a special way to create dictionaries that can change and be made as needed. It's like a special tool that helps make dictionaries in a flexible way. Key-value pairs are like pairs of things that go together, like a matching set of socks. These pairs can be used in a special way, similar to how we use lists, but with some differences. A simple example, `{x: x**2 for x in range(10)}`, creates a dictionary where each key is a number from 0 to 9, and each value is its square.

Set comprehensions, like their list and dictionary counterparts, offer a concise way to create sets. The syntax is nearly identical to list comprehensions but uses curly braces instead of square brackets. This allows for the creation of sets in a way that is both efficient and easily readable, for instance, `{x for x in 'abracadabra' if x not in 'abc'}`.

Generator expressions are closely related to list comprehensions but have the added advantage of being more memory-efficient. They are enclosed in parentheses rather than brackets or braces and are used for creating generators – a type of iterable like lists or tuples, but they generate their items on-the-fly and do not store the entire sequence in memory. This makes generator expressions particularly useful for large datasets.

The elegance of comprehensions in Python lies in their ability to condense loops and if statements into single lines of code, making the code not only more readable but also more expressive. They eliminate the need for appending to lists, dictionaries, or sets in a loop, thereby streamlining the code and enhancing its readability and performance.

In conclusion, comprehensions are a testament to Python's ability to handle data processing tasks with simplicity and elegance. They are a powerful tool in a Python programmer's toolkit, allowing for the writing of more efficient, readable, and concise code. As you delve into Python's advanced features, the use of comprehensions will undoubtedly become a staple in your coding practice, enabling you to handle data in a more efficient and Pythonic way. In simple terms, the idea behind comprehensions in Python is to make the code look nice and be easy to understand. It's like following the rule that something pretty is better than something ugly, and something simple is better than something complicated.

## Context Managers for Resource Management

In the sophisticated arena of Python's advanced features, context managers emerge as a pivotal tool for resource management. The section "Context Managers for Resource Management" in the chapter "Advanced Topics in Python" focuses on unraveling the functionality and significance of context managers. These are not just coding constructs; they embody a systematic approach for allocating and releasing resources efficiently and safely, ensuring that resources like file streams, network connections, and locks are properly managed throughout the lifecycle of a program.

The essence of a context manager in Python lies in its ability to provide a structural mechanism for managing resources, particularly in situations where setup and teardown processes are necessary. The primary motivation for using context managers is to ensure that resources are handled correctly — resources are allocated when needed and, more importantly, released when they are no longer required. This is akin to having a well-trained supervisor who ensures that all tools and resources are checked out and returned properly in a workshop, maintaining order and preventing resource leaks.

In Python, context managers are often used in file handling, where it's crucial to close a file after its content has been processed. Without context managers, a programmer might forget to close a file, leading to potential memory leaks and data corruption. When we use a context manager, it takes care of closing the file for us. It will close the file no matter what happens, even if there is an error. This automatic management of resources is the hallmark of context managers, providing both efficiency and safety in resource handling.

The implementation of context managers in Python is facilitated by the `with` statement. The `with` statement makes it easier to deal with problems by taking care of certain tasks before and after the problem occurs. A context manager is like a special helper that helps you do something in a certain way when you use a special code word called "with". It sets up the rules and conditions for how things should happen while you are doing that particular thing. This object needs to implement two methods: `__enter__()` and `__exit__()`. The `__enter__()` method is executed at the start of the block, setting up the context, and the `__exit__()` method is invoked at the end of the block, tearing down the context.

A context manager is like a helper that helps us do something. An example of a context manager is the `open()` function. It helps us open files so that we can read or write things in them. When you use `open()` in a `with` block, the file is opened when entering the block and automatically closed when exiting, regardless of whether an exception occurred. This automatic handling of files not only makes the code cleaner and more readable but also more robust and error-free.

In Python, there are special things called context managers that help us manage certain tasks. We can use ones that are already built-in, but we can also create our own custom ones if we need to. This is useful in scenarios where resources need custom setup and teardown. For instance, you might create a context manager for a network connection that ensures the connection is properly closed after its use.

Context managers also play a vital role in ensuring that multi-threaded and multi-process applications run smoothly. They can manage locks and other synchronization mechanisms, ensuring that resources are accessed in a thread-safe manner, preventing deadlocks and race conditions.

In conclusion, context managers in Python provide an elegant and efficient way of managing resources. They encapsulate resource management logic, ensuring that resources are correctly managed and released, thereby preventing resource leaks and other related issues. As you advance in Python programming, understanding and utilizing context managers will enable you to write more robust, clean, and efficient code, particularly in resource-intensive applications. They represent a sophisticated approach to resource management, aligning with Python's philosophy of simplicity and elegance in coding.

## Conclusion of Chapter 11: Advanced Topics in Python

As we conclude our journey through "Advanced Topics in Python," you now stand at a new vantage point in your Python programming journey. This chapter has equipped you with an arsenal of sophisticated tools and concepts, enabling you to tackle more complex programming challenges with confidence and creativity. The advanced features of Python discussed in this chapter are not just theoretical concepts; they are practical tools that, when mastered, can significantly enhance the quality and efficiency of your code.

The journey through decorators, iterators, generators, comprehensions, and context managers is more than an academic exercise. It's like a special way of writing instructions for computers that is not only clear and works well, but is also very clever and fast. These advanced concepts encourage you to think more deeply about your code structure, efficiency, and resource management, paving the way for you to become not just a Python programmer, but a Python craftsman.

As you move forward, let the knowledge and skills acquired in this chapter inspire you to explore even more of what Python has to offer. The journey of learning Python is continuous, and each step forward opens new doors of possibility. Embrace these advanced topics as you continue to grow and develop in your programming career, and you will find that Python offers an ever-expanding universe of opportunities to those who seek to master it.

# Exercises: Advanced Python Coding Challenges

Embark on a journey of deepening your Python expertise with these advanced coding challenges. Each exercise is designed to push the boundaries of your understanding and application of Python, particularly focusing on the advanced concepts discussed in Chapter 11, "Advanced Topics in Python". These challenges are not just tests of skill but pathways to mastering Python's more sophisticated features.

1. **Custom Decorator Creation**: Write a decorator that logs the arguments and return value of any function it decorates.
2. **Generator for Infinite Sequence**: Create a generator that produces an infinite sequence of Fibonacci numbers.
3. **Nested List Comprehension**: Use a list comprehension to flatten a nested list structure.
4. **Context Manager for File Handling**: Write a context manager for safely handling file read and write operations.
5. **Decorator for Execution Time**: Develop a decorator that measures and prints the execution time of a function.
6. **Generator Expression for Prime Numbers**: Use a generator expression to yield the first 50 prime numbers.
7. **Set Comprehension with Condition**: Create a set comprehension that includes squares of even numbers from 1 to 20.
8. **Recursive Generator Function**: Write a recursive generator function to traverse a nested data structure, such as a JSON object.
9. **Custom Iterator Class**: Implement a custom iterator that iterates over every other element in a given list.
10. **Dictionary Comprehension from Two Lists**: Use dictionary comprehension to create a dictionary from two lists, one as keys and the other as values.
11. **Decorator with Arguments**: Develop a decorator that takes arguments and modifies the behavior of the function it decorates accordingly.

12. **File Reading using Context Manager**: Create a context manager for reading a file and printing its content in uppercase.

13. **List Comprehension for Filtering Data**: Use a list comprehension to filter and process data from a list of dictionaries.

14. **Generator for Reading Large File**: Write a generator to read a large file line by line to avoid memory issues.

15. **Nested Decorators Application**: Apply multiple decorators to a single function and understand the order of their execution.

16. **Context Manager for Database Connection**: Develop a context manager for managing database connections.

17. **Creating a Chain of Generators**: Implement a chain of generators to process data through multiple stages.

18. **Advanced Set Comprehension**: Use a set comprehension to generate a set of tuples representing all possible combinations from two different sets.

19. **Dynamic Function Modification with Decorators**: Write a decorator that dynamically modifies certain aspects of a function's behavior.

20. **Efficient Data Aggregation with Generator**: Create a generator that efficiently aggregates data from multiple sources, such as files or APIs, without exhausting memory resources.

These exercises are crafted to challenge and expand your understanding of Python's advanced features, encouraging you to think creatively and write code that's not just functional, but also efficient and elegant. As you tackle these challenges, you will hone your skills in Python and gain a deeper appreciation for the language's capabilities and versatility.

# Chapter 12: Web Development Basics with Python

**Introduction to Chapter 12: Web Development Basics with Python**

Welcome to "Web Development Basics with Python," a chapter that serves as your gateway into the world of creating dynamic and interactive web applications using Python. This chapter is designed to transform your understanding of Python from a scripting or backend language to a powerful tool for web development. Python, with its simplicity and versatility, has extended its reach into the web development domain, offering frameworks like Flask and Django to create feature-rich web applications.

In this journey, you'll first encounter web frameworks, diving into the nuances of Flask and Django, understanding their architecture, and how they equip you to build robust web applications. Then, you'll take the practical route of building your first web application. This hands-on experience is really important because it helps connect what we learn in books to how we use it in the real world.

Moving forward, the chapter delves into the integral components of web development – Templates, Routing, and Web Forms. These elements are like the bricks that are used to build a house. They help make websites work and look nice for people to use. You'll learn how to craft user interfaces with templates, manage application routes, and create interactive forms for user input. This way of learning makes sure you understand everything about making websites with Python. It covers all the important parts.

As you start learning about web development with Python, remember that it's not just about writing code. It's about making things that people can use and enjoy, finding solutions to problems, and connecting people with technology.

# Introduction to Web Frameworks (Flask, Django)

In the dynamic world of web development, Python emerges as a robust language, offering powerful and versatile frameworks like Flask and Django. The section "Introduction to Web Frameworks (Flask, Django)" in the chapter "Web Development Basics with Python" is designed to provide a foundational understanding of these two prominent frameworks. They are not merely tools for building web applications; they represent distinct philosophies and approaches in the web development landscape, each with its unique strengths and use cases.

Flask, often celebrated for its simplicity and elegance, is a micro-framework. We call it a 'micro' framework because it is designed to be small and easy to understand, but also allows us to add more features if we want to. Flask provides the bare essentials for web development, offering route declarations and view functions. The beauty of Flask lies in its lightweight and modular design, allowing developers to use only what they need, while having the flexibility to plug in numerous extensions for added functionalities like form validation, user authentication, database integration, and more.

An example to understand Flask can be akin to building a custom car from scratch. You start with a basic chassis and engine, and then you add components according to your specific needs and preferences. Flask is particularly well-suited for small to medium-sized web applications and for developers who prefer a 'DIY' approach to web development.

Django is like a special tool for building websites using the Python programming language. It helps people make websites quickly and with a neat and organized design. Django is like a special tool that helps people who want to make things perfect, but also need to finish their work quickly. It follows the "batteries-included" philosophy, providing almost everything developers need right out of the box. This includes an ORM (Object-Relational Mapper), an admin panel, a templating engine, form handling, authentication support, and more.

To understand Django, imagine constructing a building with prefabricated modules. Each module is a fully functional component like a kitchen, a bathroom, or a living room. You just need to select and arrange these modules to build your house quickly and efficiently. Django is ideal for developers who want to create large-scale, feature-rich web applications and wish to focus more on writing the app itself rather than the underlying infrastructure.

Both Flask and Django are built on Python, which means they benefit from Python's readability and simplicity. Choosing between Flask and Django often depends on the requirements of the web application you're looking to develop and your personal or your team's preference in terms of flexibility and control versus convenience and feature-completeness.

In conclusion, understanding Flask and Django is crucial for any Python developer looking to venture into web development. These frameworks make it easier to create websites and web applications. Instead of starting from scratch, you can use these frameworks to help you build your app faster. As you delve into Flask and Django, you will appreciate their unique philosophies – Flask's minimalism and flexibility, and Django's all-encompassing, feature-rich approach. Both frameworks open doors to the vast world of web development, offering powerful tools to transform your ideas into fully-functioning web applications.

# Building Your First Web Application

Embarking on the journey of building your first web application with Python is an exciting venture, a blend of creativity, logic, and technology. The section "Building Your First Web Application" in the chapter "Web Development Basics with Python" is designed to be your roadmap through this adventure. Building a web application is not just about coding; it's about bringing an idea to life, making it accessible over the web, and creating an interactive experience for users.

To begin making your web application, the first thing you need to do is learn about how web applications are organized. A web application is like a game you play with your friend. You are the client and your friend is the server. You send requests to your friend, and they send back responses to help you play the game. The client is typically a web browser that requests information, and the server is where your application resides, processing those requests and sending responses back. When you use the internet, the client (like your computer or phone) talks to the server (a big computer that stores information) using a special language called HTTP.

Now, let's delve into the practical steps of building a simple web application. For this journey, we will use Flask, given its simplicity and elegance for beginners. Flask allows you to set up a web server with minimal hassle and write your web application's logic using Python.

1. **Setting Up the Environment**: First, you need to set up your development environment. This involves installing Python and Flask. You can install Flask using pip, Python's package manager, with the command `pip install Flask`.

2. **Creating a Basic Flask Application**: Start by creating a new Python file, say `app.py`. This file will contain the code for your web application. Begin by importing Flask, and then create an instance of the Flask class. This instance will be your WSGI (Web Server Gateway Interface) application.

```
from flash import Flask
app = Flask(_ _name_ _)
```

3. **Defining Routes and Views**: In Flask, you define routes using decorators. A route is a URL pattern that the application will handle. Below each route, you define a view function, which returns the content for that URL.

```
@app.route('/')
def home():
    Return 'Hello, World!'
```

This code creates a route for the home page (`'/'`) and defines a view function `home` that returns a simple message.

4. **Running the Flask Application**: To run the application, you tell Flask to run the app with `app.run()`. This starts a local web server.

```
if __name__ == '__main__':
    app.run(debug=True)
```

The `debug=True` argument enables Flask's debugger, so you get a helpful debug page if something goes wrong.

5. **Accessing Your Web Application**: Once the server is running, you can access your web application by going to `http://127.0.0.1:5000/` in your web browser. You should see the 'Hello, World!' message.

As you progress, you'll expand your application by adding more routes, handling different types of requests, and returning more complex responses. You'll learn to render HTML templates, process user input from web forms, and interact with a database.

In conclusion, building your first web application with Python and Flask is a journey of learning and exploration. It requires understanding the basics of web servers, HTTP, and Flask, but the result is rewarding. As you develop your web application, you will gain practical skills in web development, which form the foundation for more complex applications in the future. This project is not just about coding; it's about bringing your ideas to the web and making them interactively available to users worldwide.

# Templates, Routing, and Web Forms

Diving into web development with Python, especially with frameworks like Flask and Django, introduces three critical components – Templates, Routing, and Web Forms. This section of "Web Development Basics with Python" is dedicated to unraveling these elements, which are fundamental to building dynamic, interactive web applications. Far from being just coding aspects, they represent the bridge between your application's backend logic and the user's interface, ensuring a seamless and interactive web experience.

**Templates: Crafting the User Interface**

In the realm of web development, templates are the cornerstone of building user interfaces. They are essentially blueprint files, usually written in HTML, which are used to generate dynamic web pages. Templates separate the presentation of your application from its Python logic. In frameworks like Flask and Django, templating engines like Jinja2 are used, which allow for embedding Python-like expressions directly within HTML.

Imagine templates as the canvas where you paint your website's layout. They define how the webpage will look, but they are brought to life by the data passed into them from your Python application. This separation of concerns not only makes your code cleaner and more maintainable but also allows for designers and developers to work in tandem more effectively.

Creating a template usually involves defining placeholders for dynamic content that will be filled with real data when the page is rendered. This might include user details, list of items, or any other data your application manages. Templates can also extend and include other templates, allowing for reusable layout pieces like headers, footers, and navigation bars.

**Routing: Connecting Requests to Responses**

Routing is the mechanism by which HTTP requests are connected to the Python code that handles them. Each route is associated with a URL pattern, and when Flask or Django receives a request that matches a particular pattern, it invokes the corresponding view function. This view function processes the request, interacts with the database or other backend services if necessary, and returns a response, often using a template.

Understanding routing is like understanding the roadmap of a city. Just as different addresses take you to different locations, different URL patterns lead the user to different parts of your web application. Routes can also capture parameters from URLs, allowing for dynamic behavior based on user input, such as displaying a specific profile page or blog post.

**Web Forms: Interacting with Users**

Web forms are a vital aspect of user interaction in web applications. They allow users to submit data to your web application, ranging from simple text inputs to complex data structures. In Python web frameworks, forms are typically handled by defining a form class, which specifies the fields and their types, such as text, date, or dropdown selections.

Handling web forms involves receiving the form data submitted by the user, validating it, and processing it. Validation is really important because it helps us check if the information, we receive is true, accurate, and safe to use. After validation, the application can respond accordingly, such as saving the data to a database, performing a calculation, or redirecting the user to another page.

Web forms are the interactive elements of your application. They are the means by which users can communicate, input data, and configure options. It's really important to be able to fill out forms on the internet quickly and safely so that we can have a good and safe time using websites.

In conclusion, templates, routing, and web forms are the trifecta of building web applications with Python. Templates allow you to define the structure and appearance of your web pages, routing connects user requests to the appropriate Python logic, and web forms facilitate user interaction and data input. Together, these components enable you to build dynamic, interactive, and user-friendly web applications. As you explore these areas, you will develop a deeper understanding of how web applications work and how to harness Python's power to create your own.

**Conclusion of Chapter 12: Web Development Basics with Python**

As we conclude "Web Development Basics with Python," you stand at a significant milestone in your journey as a Python developer. This chapter has not only introduced you to the world of web development using Python but has also equipped you with the essential skills to build your own web applications. From understanding the framework architectures of Flask and Django to the practical experience of constructing a web application and mastering templates, routing, and web forms, you now possess a solid foundation in web development.

Learning web development is like going on a never-ending adventure that keeps changing and growing. The skills you've acquired in this chapter form the bedrock upon which you can build more complex and sophisticated web applications. The world of web development is always changing and getting better. As a web developer, you will always be learning new things and adjusting to new ways of doing things.

Welcome and accept the difficult and exciting things that come with making websites. Use your newfound skills to experiment, create, and innovate. Python's flexibility and the power of its web frameworks provide a canvas for you to bring your ideas to life. As you keep getting better, keep trying new things, keep learning, and keep trying to do more with Python in making websites.

## Exercises: Creating Basic Web Applications

As you delve into the world of web development with Python, practical exercises are crucial in consolidating your learning and enhancing your skillset. The "Exercises: Creating Basic Web Applications" section in the chapter "12. Web Development Basics with Python" presents a series of hands-on challenges designed to apply your knowledge in real-world scenarios. These exercises will guide you through the nuances of web application development, from simple projects to more complex tasks.

1. **Hello World Flask App**: Create a basic Flask application that displays 'Hello, World!' on the home page.
2. **Personal Web Page with Django**: Using Django, build a personal webpage that includes a biography and a photo gallery.
3. **Flask Blog Post Route**: Implement a route in a Flask app that displays a blog post based on a unique ID in the URL.
4. **Django Contact Form**: Create a contact form in Django that captures user name, email, and message, and displays the submitted data on a new page.
5. **Temperature Conversion Tool**: Develop a Flask app that converts temperatures between Celsius and Fahrenheit.
6. **Django ToDo List**: Build a simple ToDo list application in Django that allows users to add, edit, and delete tasks.
7. **Flask URL Shortener**: Create a Flask application that shortens URLs and redirects users to the original URL when the short link is visited.

8. **User Registration Form in Django**: Implement a user registration form in Django with fields like username, password, email, and date of birth.

9. **Flask Data Visualization**: Use Flask to display a simple chart created from hard-coded data.

10. **Django Polling App**: Build a polling application in Django where users can vote on different topics.

11. **Book Review Platform with Flask**: Create a Flask app where users can post book reviews and rate books.

12. **Django Movie Database**: Develop a movie database application in Django with search functionality.

13. **Flask Email Sender**: Make a Flask app that sends emails using a form with fields like recipient, subject, and message.

14. **Restaurant Menu App in Django**: Create an app in Django for displaying a restaurant's menu with different categories.

15. **Flask Image Gallery**: Build a simple image gallery application in Flask where users can upload and view images.

16. **Django Event Calendar**: Develop an event calendar application in Django that allows users to add and view events.

17. **Flask File Uploader**: Implement a file uploader in Flask that allows users to upload files and then displays a list of uploaded files.

18. **Django Blog with Comments**: Create a blog application in Django that supports posting articles and user comments.

19. **Flask Location-Based App**: Develop an app in Flask that takes a location input from the user and displays relevant information about the area.

20. **Django Library Management System**: Build a simple library management system in Django for tracking book loans and returns.

These exercises cover a broad range of functionalities, from basic web pages to dynamic content management. As you work through these challenges, you'll gain hands-on experience with both Flask and Django, enhancing your understanding of web development concepts and preparing you for more advanced web development projects.

# Chapter 13: Python for Data Science and Machine Learning

**Introduction to Chapter 13: Python for Data Science and Machine Learning**

Welcome to "Python for Data Science and Machine Learning," a chapter that signifies a pivotal turn into the fascinating world where data tells stories and algorithms predict the future. Python, a language revered for its simplicity and power, is at the forefront of this revolution, offering tools and libraries that transform data into insights. This chapter is a journey through the core aspects of data science and machine learning, tailored to provide you with a comprehensive understanding of how Python is applied in these rapidly evolving fields.

Embark on this exploration by delving into the world of Pandas for data analysis, where data is cleaned, processed, and prepared. Then, transition into the realm of data visualization with Matplotlib and Seaborn, bringing data to life through powerful graphical representations. Following this, you will be introduced to the fundamentals of machine learning with Scikit-Learn, a library that demystifies complex algorithms and makes machine learning accessible and practical.

This chapter is not just about learning tools and techniques; it's about acquiring a mindset. A mindset that sees data as more than numbers and figures, and machine learning as more than algorithms and models. This is about learning how to use Python to find important information in data and make smart guesses about what will happen.

# Data Analysis with Pandas

In the landscape of Python programming, Pandas stands out as a cornerstone for data analysis and manipulation. The segment "Data Analysis with Pandas" in the chapter "Python for Data Science and Machine Learning" is designed to walk you through the capabilities of this powerful library. Pandas is not just a tool; it's a gateway to handling and understanding data, allowing for sophisticated manipulation and analysis with ease and efficiency.

Pandas is a tool that helps us work with numbers and organize them in tables. It also helps us work with time-related information. This thing called DataFrame is really famous because it helps you work with data in a special way. It lets you organize and change data that looks like a table with rows and columns.

**Understanding DataFrames and Series**

A DataFrame is like a table with rows and columns, where you can put different types of information. You can change the size of the table and the information in it. Imagine you have a piece of paper with rows and columns on it. Each row represents something different, like a person or an item, and each column represents a specific detail about that thing, like their name or their age. In Python, we can create something similar called a spreadsheet or SQL table, where we can store and organize information in a structured way. A DataFrame is like a table, and each column in the table is like a list. A list is a collection of things, like numbers or words, and it can hold different types of things. Pandas is great because it can easily do things with rows and columns at the same time. A DataFrame is like a box that holds many smaller boxes called Series.

**Data Loading and Inspection**

Pandas excel in loading data from various sources like CSV files, SQL databases, or JSON files. Once data is loaded into a DataFrame, Pandas provides numerous functions for quick data inspection. Methods like `.head()`, `.tail()`, `.info()`, and `.describe()` offer a glimpse into the nature and structure of your data, providing insights on data types, missing values, and statistical summaries.

**Data Cleaning and Preparation**

In real-world data analysis, data rarely comes clean. Pandas provides a suite of tools for handling missing data, duplicate data, string manipulation, and date parsing. Functions like `.fillna()`, `.drop_duplicates()`, and `.apply()` enable you to clean and transform your data frames, preparing them for analysis.

**Data Filtering and Selection**

Selecting and filtering data is a frequent task in data analysis. Pandas enables efficient slicing, indexing, and subsetting of data. You can filter data using column names, conditional statements, or Pandas' `.query()` method. Whether it's selecting specific columns or filtering rows based on a condition, Pandas makes the process intuitive and efficient.

**Grouping and Aggregation**

Pandas truly shines when it comes to grouping and aggregating data. The `.groupby()` method allows you to group data on certain criteria and perform operations like summing, averaging, or counting. This feature is really important for looking at information and finding out how things are changing and repeating. It helps us see patterns and understand what is happening.

## Merging, Joining, and Concatenating

Sometimes, you need to put together information from different places. Pandas facilitates this with functions like `.merge()`, `.join()`, and `.concat()`. These functions provide the ability to horizontally or vertically combine DataFrames, similar to SQL join operations.

## Time Series Analysis

Pandas is a tool that can help us work with data that changes over time. It can do many things like creating a list of dates, changing the time period of data, calculating statistics based on a certain time period, moving data forward or backward in time, and looking at data from the past. The ease of handling time series data with Pandas is unparalleled.

## Visualization Integration

Pandas seamlessly integrates with Matplotlib for data visualization, offering a familiar and easy way to generate plots, histograms, scatter matrices, and more, right from DataFrame and Series objects.

To sum it up, Pandas is like an important tool that helps scientists who use Python to work with data. This tool is really useful for people who work with data. It can help them change and understand the data in different ways. It's something that they really need to do their job well. As you dive into Pandas, you'll discover a world where data is not just numbers and text but a narrative waiting to be explored and understood. Pandas doesn't just help you analyze data; it helps you weave the story hidden within the data.

# Data Visualization: Matplotlib and Seaborn

In the realm of Python's data science toolkit, data visualization stands as a critical component, bringing data to life through graphical representation. The segment "Data Visualization: Matplotlib and Seaborn" in the chapter "Python for Data Science and Machine Learning" delves into two of Python's most popular visualization libraries: Matplotlib and Seaborn. These tools do more than just paint a pretty picture; they enable the transformation of complex data sets into comprehensible and insightful visual narratives, essential for data analysis and decision-making.

**Matplotlib: The Foundation of Python Visualization**

Matplotlib, often considered the grandfather of Python visualization libraries, is a versatile and powerful tool for creating static, interactive, and animated visualizations in Python. This is a tool that helps to create pictures and put them into different computer programs using tools like Tkinter, wxPython, Qt, or GTK.

The strength of Matplotlib lies in its ability to offer fine-grained control over virtually every element of a plot or chart, from the size of the figures to the exact placement of elements on the plot. This level of control makes it an excellent tool for creating precise scientific graphs and charts for publication.

Matplotlib operates on a straightforward principle: creating a figure, creating one or more plots or axes on the figure, and then plotting data on the axes. This approach provides a familiar environment for those coming from a MATLAB background, but it can also be somewhat cumbersome for everyday use. This is where the library's versatility shines, as it offers several ways to interact with its API, from the Pyplot module for MATLAB-style functionality to a more Pythonic object-oriented approach.

# Seaborn: Statistical Data Visualization

While Matplotlib is powerful, it can sometimes require extensive code for complex visualizations, and this is where Seaborn enters the scene. Seaborn is like a fancy version of Matplotlib that makes it easier to create pretty pictures that show information about numbers and patterns. It's particularly well-suited for exploring and understanding complex datasets and for creating graphics that can uncover hidden aspects of the data.

Seaborn makes it easier to create really cool pictures that show information in a simple way, like maps that show hot and cold places, graphs that show how things change over time, and pictures that show how things are spread out. It works well with Pandas DataFrames, which is really helpful for analyzing data. Seaborn's plotting functions operate on entire dataframes and arrays, automatically aggregating and summarizing the data for effective visualization.

One of Seaborn's standout features is its beautiful default styles and color palettes, which make the creation of aesthetically pleasing charts and graphs almost effortless. It also simplifies the creation of complex visualizations like pair plots and joint plots, which can be useful for machine learning tasks.

## Integration and Use Cases

Both Matplotlib and Seaborn can be used for a wide range of tasks: from creating simple bar charts and line plots to more complex scatter plots and heatmaps. They are indispensable tools for exploratory data analysis, helping to identify trends, patterns, and outliers in data. In machine learning, these visualizations are crucial for understanding the distribution of data, the relationships between features, and the performance of models.

In conclusion, Matplotlib and Seaborn are pivotal in the Python data visualization landscape. While Matplotlib provides the foundation and granular control, Seaborn extends its capabilities, focusing on the ease of use and aesthetic presentation. Together, they form a powerful duo for data scientists and analysts, turning complex data into visual stories that are easy to understand and compelling to explore. As you embark on data visualization tasks in Python, mastering these libraries will not only aid in your data analysis but also in effectively communicating your findings and insights.

# Introduction to Machine Learning with Scikit-Learn

In the burgeoning world of Python's application in data science and machine learning, Scikit-Learn emerges as a beacon for those beginning their journey into machine learning (ML). The segment "Introduction to Machine Learning with Scikit-Learn" in the chapter "Python for Data Science and Machine Learning" is tailored to unfold the essentials of Scikit-Learn, a library that offers simplicity and versatility for machine learning tasks. This introduction isn't just about learning a library; it's about embracing an approach that demystifies the complexities of machine learning, making it accessible and practical.

**The Genesis of Scikit-Learn**

Scikit-Learn is like a special tool that helps computers learn new things. It is made up of other tools called NumPy, SciPy, and Matplotlib. It is a popular library for machine learning, which is when computers learn from data. It was created to make it easier for different learning machines to talk to each other and work together. The beauty of Scikit-Learn lies in its well-structured and easy-to-follow framework, which makes machine learning approachable for beginners, yet robust enough for seasoned practitioners.

## Core Features of Scikit-Learn

Scikit-Learn is renowned for its comprehensive collection of tools for data preprocessing, supervised and unsupervised learning, model selection, evaluation, and more. The library's functionalities are neatly organized into modules like `sklearn.preprocessing` for data preprocessing, `sklearn.linear_model` for linear models, `sklearn.cluster` for clustering algorithms, and so on.

## Machine Learning Basics with Scikit-Learn

Understanding machine learning with Scikit-Learn begins with grasping the fundamental concepts and processes in machine learning. Then there are different tasks that computers can do with what they learn. Classification is when the computer puts things into different groups based on what it has learned. Regression is when the computer tries to predict a number or value based on what it has learned. This means learning about different ways that computers can learn. There are two main types: supervised and unsupervised learning. Supervised learning is like having a teacher that guides the computer and tells it if it's doing something right or wrong. Unsupervised learning is like the computer figuring things out on its own without any guidance. Lastly, it's also important to divide the information into two sets: training and test sets. The training set is like practicing what the computer has learned, and the test set is like a test to see how well the computer has learned. Another important thing is featuring extraction, which means finding the most important parts of the information the computer is learning from. It's like finding the key parts of a story.

## Supervised Learning: The Starting Point

For beginners, Scikit-Learn offers an ideal playground to start with supervised learning tasks, where the goal is to learn a mapping from inputs to outputs based on example input-output pairs. The library has different methods for solving problems, like predicting numbers, classifying things, making decisions, and creating random groupings. Each method is good for different types of problems.

## Unsupervised Learning: Exploring the Unlabeled

Unsupervised learning in Scikit-Learn involves working with algorithms to analyze and cluster unlabeled datasets. These algorithms are like detectives that find secret clues or special shapes in information that we give them. Scikit-Learn includes clustering methods like K-Means, hierarchical clustering, and DBSCAN, and dimensionality reduction techniques like PCA (Principal Component Analysis) and t-SNE.

## Model Evaluation and Improvement

Scikit-Learn excels in offering tools for evaluating and improving machine learning models. This includes cross-validation techniques, metrics for performance assessment, and utilities for tuning model parameters. It's really important to know how to use these tools because it helps us make models that are not only correct, but also strong and can be used in different situations.

## Practical Examples and Applications

To fully grasp the capabilities of Scikit-Learn, practical examples and applications are essential. For instance, employing Scikit-Learn to create a model for predicting house prices using a dataset with various features or clustering a dataset of articles into different topics.

In simple terms, Scikit-Learn is like a very important building block in the world of machine learning using Python. It helps people create and use different tools and techniques to make computers learn and make decisions on their own. It's like a special collection of tools that is easy to use and can be used by both beginners and experts in machine learning. As you delve into the realms of Scikit-Learn, you embark on a journey that not only teaches you the mechanics of various machine learning algorithms but also guides you in applying these techniques to solve real-world problems effectively. The journey through Scikit-Learn is as much about learning the syntax as it is about understanding the strategic approach to machine learning.

## Conclusion of Chapter 13: Python for Data Science and Machine Learning

As we conclude this chapter, "Python for Data Science and Machine Learning," you stand at the threshold of a new world where data drives decisions, and predictive algorithms shape the future. This chapter has equipped you with the foundational tools and knowledge to embark on your journey in data science and machine learning with Python. From understanding the nuances of data manipulation with Pandas to creating compelling visualizations and diving into the mechanics of machine learning models, you are now better prepared to tackle the challenges and opportunities that lie in the vast expanse of data science.

The journey of learning about data science and machine learning never stops and is always changing and growing. New things are always being discovered and invented in the field. Stay curious, keep exploring, and continue to build upon the skills you've acquired. The path ahead is not just about applying what you've learned; it's about innovating, experimenting, and contributing to this dynamic field.

Embrace the power of Python as your tool for exploring and making sense of the complex world of data. Let your journey in data science and machine learning be guided by a pursuit of knowledge, a passion for discovery, and a vision to transform data into actionable insights. This chapter is just the beginning, and the future is yours to shape.

# Exercises: Data Science Mini-Projects

The "Exercises: Data Science Mini-Projects" section in the chapter "13. Python for Data Science and Machine Learning" offers a series of engaging and insightful mini-projects. These exercises are designed to harness and expand your understanding of Python in the realms of data science and machine learning. Each project provides a hands-on experience, reinforcing the concepts learned and applying them to real-world scenarios.

1. **Housing Price Analysis**: Using the Pandas library, analyze a dataset of housing prices, exploring factors that influence prices the most.
2. **Visualizing Climate Change**: Create a series of visualizations using Matplotlib and Seaborn to depict the impact of climate change over the past few decades.
3. **Email Spam Filter**: Build a basic email spam classifier using Scikit-Learn's machine learning models.
4. **Social Media Trend Analysis**: Utilize Pandas to analyze social media data, identifying trending topics and sentiment analysis.
5. **Stock Market Prediction**: Implement a simple linear regression model to predict stock prices.
6. **Customer Segmentation with K-Means**: Use Scikit-Learn to perform customer segmentation analysis for a retail dataset.
7. **Movie Recommendation System**: Create a basic recommendation system using a movies dataset.
8. **Analyzing Healthcare Data**: Explore a healthcare dataset to identify patterns and insights using Pandas and visualization libraries.

9. **Predicting Credit Card Fraud**: Implement a machine learning model to detect potential credit card fraud.

10. **Text Analysis of a Novel**: Perform a text analysis on a novel or a collection of texts, identifying key themes and patterns.

11. **Sales Forecasting Model**: Develop a model to forecast sales data for the next quarter using time series analysis.

12. **Analyzing Sports Data**: Use sports data to analyze player performance, team trends, and predict future outcomes.

13. **Interactive Dashboard for Data Analysis**: Build an interactive dashboard using Python libraries for real-time data analysis.

14. **Image Classification with Machine Learning**: Create a simple image classification model to categorize different objects.

15. **Sentiment Analysis of Reviews**: Analyze customer reviews from an e-commerce platform to gauge overall sentiment.

16. **Real Estate Valuation Model**: Develop a model to estimate the value of real estate properties based on various features.

17. **Analyzing Public Health Data**: Explore a public health dataset to uncover insights and trends in health metrics.

18. **Flight Delay Prediction**: Predict flight delays using historical flight data and weather information.

19. **Music Genre Classification**: Classify music into different genres based on their features using a machine learning model.

20. **Biodiversity Data Analysis**: Analyze a dataset related to biodiversity, examining species distribution and conservation status.

These mini-projects not only enhance your practical skills but also deepen your understanding of how data science and machine learning can be applied to solve diverse problems. As you work through these projects, you will experience the power of Python in transforming data into meaningful insights and predictions, preparing you for more advanced challenges in your data science journey.

# Chapter 14: The Road Ahead: Becoming a Python Expert

**Introduction to Chapter 14: The Road Ahead: Becoming a Python Expert**

Welcome to the final chapter, "The Road Ahead: Becoming a Python Expert," a comprehensive guide that marks the culmination of your journey in Python. This chapter is more than just a summary; it's a roadmap to the future, outlining the steps to take as you transition from proficiency to mastery in Python. Python is not just a programming language; it's a vast ecosystem that offers endless possibilities for those willing to delve deeper. This chapter is designed to open those doors, guiding you through advanced libraries and frameworks, highlighting the significance of community engagement and open-source contributions, and exploring the myriad of career opportunities that await you.

As you embark on this chapter, you'll explore the complex and powerful tools that lie beyond the basics, diving into libraries that push the boundaries of what you can achieve with Python. It's really important to be a part of the Python community, where people who use and love Python come together. By contributing to open-source projects, which means sharing your ideas and work with others, you can help make Python even better. And it's also important to keep learning and growing with the language, so you can always be up to date with the latest and coolest things you can do with Python. The journey through this chapter will illuminate the path to harnessing the full potential of Python, preparing you to tackle more challenging problems and to take on roles that shape the future of technology.

## Exploring Further: Advanced Libraries and Frameworks

As you journey along "The Road Ahead: Becoming a Python Expert," a pivotal chapter in your odyssey with Python, we approach a crucial milestone: "Exploring Further: Advanced Libraries and Frameworks." This segment is not merely about learning new tools; it's about expanding your horizon, deepening your understanding, and embracing the sophistication that Python offers. It's about exploring the uncharted territories of Python's capabilities and integrating them into your skillset to solve complex problems and innovate.

**The Landscape of Advanced Python Libraries**

The Python ecosystem is vast and diverse, with libraries and frameworks for virtually every task and industry. From web development to scientific computing, from machine learning to data visualization, Python's advanced libraries are the engines powering today's tech innovations.

1. **Web Development – Beyond Flask and Django**: Explore advanced web frameworks like Pyramid and Falcon, which offer more flexibility and scalability for complex web applications.

2. **Asynchronous Programming with Asyncio**: Dive into the world of asynchronous programming with Asyncio, a library that allows you to write concurrent code using the async/await syntax, making your Python applications more efficient.

3. **Scientific Computing with SciPy and NumPy**: Venture deeper into the realms of scientific computing. SciPy and NumPy are foundational libraries for scientific computations, providing tools and techniques for numerical integration, optimization, and matrix operations.

4. **Data Manipulation with Advanced Pandas**: Elevate your data manipulation skills with advanced features of Pandas. Explore time series analysis, multi-level indexing, and efficient data aggregation.

5. **Machine Learning with TensorFlow and PyTorch**: Go beyond Scikit-Learn and explore TensorFlow and PyTorch, libraries that offer more flexibility and power for building complex machine learning models, including deep learning architectures.

6. **Natural Language Processing with NLTK and SpaCy**: Step into the world of natural language processing (NLP) with NLTK and SpaCy, unlocking the ability to analyze, understand, and generate human language.

7. **Data Visualization with Plotly and Bokeh**: Enhance your data visualization skills with Plotly and Bokeh, libraries that enable the creation of interactive and aesthetically pleasing charts and graphs.

8. **Network Analysis with NetworkX**: Discover the power of network analysis with NetworkX, a library designed to study the structure, dynamics, and functions of complex networks.

9. **Quantum Computing with Qiskit**: Embark on the cutting-edge field of quantum computing with Qiskit, a library that allows you to design quantum algorithms and run them on quantum computers.

10. **Robotics Programming with ROS**: Foray into the world of robotics with the Robot Operating System (ROS), a flexible framework for writing robot software.

**Embracing the Advanced Frameworks**

Exploring these libraries and frameworks is not just about adding more tools to your toolkit. It's about developing a deeper understanding of what's possible with Python. It means being really good at using the newest technology and using Python's abilities to do really cool and exciting things.

In conclusion, as you step into this phase of advanced libraries and frameworks, you are not just learning; you are evolving. You are transitioning from a Python programmer to a Python expert. This journey will be challenging, filled with new concepts and paradigms, but it will be rewarding. You will be equipped to tackle complex problems, contribute to cutting-edge fields, and be a part of the community that shapes the future of technology. As you explore these advanced libraries and frameworks, remember that each new library you learn, each new framework you explore, is a step closer to mastering the art and science of Python programming.

## Community Engagement and Open-Source Contributions

As you embark on the journey to becoming a Python expert, the path is not just paved with advanced coding skills and theoretical knowledge. A crucial aspect, often the lifeblood of thriving in the Python ecosystem, is community engagement and open-source contributions. The segment "Community Engagement and Open-Source Contributions" in the chapter "The Road Ahead: Becoming a Python Expert" isn't just about coding; it's about becoming part of a global movement, a community of developers dedicated to sharing knowledge and building software collaboratively.

### The Essence of Community in Python

The Python community is a diverse, global network of developers, ranging from beginners to seasoned experts. It's a community characterized by its welcoming nature, readiness to help, and a shared passion for Python. Engaging with this community means more than just learning from others; it involves sharing your knowledge, participating in discussions, and growing together.

1. **Forums and Discussion Platforms**: Engage in platforms like Stack Overflow, Reddit's r/Python, or Python's mailing lists. Share your knowledge by answering questions, or seek guidance on complex issues.

2. **Local Meetups and User Groups**: Python has a wide range of local user groups and meetups worldwide. These gatherings are invaluable for networking, learning from real-world experiences, and finding mentors or collaborators.

3. **Python Conferences**: Events like PyCon, EuroPython, and regional PyConferences offer a wealth of knowledge through talks, workshops, and tutorials. They're also an excellent opportunity for networking and understanding the latest trends in Python.

**Open-Source Contributions: Beyond Code**

Contributing to open source is a cornerstone of the Python experience. Contributing to something bigger than yourself means working together with others to make something great. Open-source contributions can be more than just writing code. Documentation, bug reporting, feature requests, and community support are equally important.

1. **Contributing Code**: Start with smaller contributions to familiar projects. Fix bugs, add small features, or refactor code. In order to contribute to a project, you need to follow some rules and use a special tool called Git to keep track of your work.

2. **Documentation**: Good documentation is crucial for open-source projects. Contribute by writing tutorials, improving how-to guides, or clarifying API documentation.

3. **Issue Reporting and Triage**: Engage by reporting bugs and participating in the issue triage process. This involves reproducing bugs, confirming bug reports, and helping maintainers understand issues better.

4. **Reviewing Pull Requests**: Once familiar with a project, start reviewing others' pull requests. Provide constructive feedback and help maintainers manage the influx of contributions.

### The Impact of Open-Source Contributions

Contributing to open-source projects has a multifaceted impact. It helps you gain exposure to different coding styles and project architectures. It hones your skills in reading and understanding large codebases. More importantly, it builds your reputation in the community, opening doors for career opportunities.

In conclusion, community engagement and open-source contributions are integral to becoming a Python expert. They help you feel like you are part of a group and encourage everyone to get better together. They also help you try new things and see how much you can do with Python. These engagements are a two-way street; you give back to the community, and in return, you grow both as a developer and a collaborator. As you step into the world of Python community engagement and open source, remember that every question you answer, every line of code you commit, and every interaction you have, contributes to your journey of becoming a Python expert.

# Career Opportunities and Continuous Learning

In the dynamic world of technology, mastering Python opens doors to a myriad of career opportunities and necessitates a commitment to continuous learning. The segment "Career Opportunities and Continuous Learning" in the chapter "The Road Ahead: Becoming a Python Expert" isn't just about identifying job roles; it's a deep dive into understanding how Python expertise can shape your career path and the importance of perpetual growth and adaptation in this ever-evolving field.

**Python's Versatility in the Job Market**

Python's versatility makes it a sought-after skill in various domains. Whether it's web development, data science, artificial intelligence, cybersecurity, or automation, Python finds its application in numerous fields, making Python experts valuable assets across diverse industries.

1. **Data Science and Analytics**: Python's extensive libraries like Pandas, NumPy, and Scikit-Learn make it a staple in data analysis and machine learning roles. As a Python expert, you can delve into roles like Data Scientist, Machine Learning Engineer, or Data Analyst, working on data modeling, predictive analysis, and algorithm development.

2. **Web Development**: With frameworks like Django and Flask, Python is also a robust tool for web development. Python developers can build server-side web applications, APIs, and microservices, contributing to the backend development of websites and applications.

3. **Automation and Scripting**: Python is renowned for its ease of automation and scripting. From simple automation scripts to complex system integrations, Python's readability and efficiency make it ideal for roles that focus on improving workflows and productivity.

4. **Academic and Scientific Research**: In scientific and academic research, Python's ability to handle and visualize large datasets and its integration with tools like Jupyter Notebooks make it essential for researchers in fields like bioinformatics, physics, and quantitative finance.

**The Pathway to Continuous Learning**

In a place where things are always changing, it's important to keep learning so you can keep up and do well in your job. Python's evolving ecosystem requires you to be on the cutting edge of new libraries, frameworks, and best practices.

1. **Online Courses and Certifications**: Engage in lifelong learning through online courses, webinars, and certification programs. Platforms like Coursera, Udacity, and edX offer courses on advanced Python topics, new libraries, and specialized fields like AI and cloud computing.

2. **Contribute and Learn**: Engage in open-source projects and community forums. Contributing to open-source projects or solving problems on platforms like Stack Overflow and GitHub not only enhances your skills but also keeps you updated with the latest trends and practices.

3. **Networking and Conferences**: Attend Python conferences, meetups, and workshops. These events are awesome chances to learn from really smart people, find out about new cool stuff, and meet and talk with experts in the field.

4. **Reading and Research**: Stay informed by reading relevant blogs, articles, and research papers. Read magazines and websites about Python and follow the news about technology to stay updated on the newest things happening.

## Integrating Career Growth with Continuous Learning

Your journey as a Python expert in the job market should intertwine with your commitment to lifelong learning. As you climb the career ladder, let your learning curve ascend simultaneously. Whether transitioning into new roles, taking up challenging projects, or leading teams, the breadth of your knowledge and the depth of your expertise will be pivotal in your career trajectory.

In conclusion, as a Python expert, your career opportunities are vast and varied. However, these opportunities are best leveraged with a commitment to continuous learning. This adventure is not just about making your resume look better; it's about learning to keep growing, being curious, and being able to change and adapt. The road ahead as a Python expert is one of perpetual development, where each step forward in learning is a step towards new horizons in your professional life.

## Conclusion of Chapter 14: The Road Ahead: Becoming a Python Expert

As we conclude "The Road Ahead: Becoming a Python Expert," you stand at a significant milestone, equipped with the knowledge, skills, and insights to forge ahead in your Python journey. This chapter has not only expanded your technical expertise but also opened your eyes to the broader landscape of Python – a landscape filled with opportunities for growth, innovation, and contribution. Becoming really good at Python is not like going in a straight line, it's more like a never-ending adventure of learning new things, trying them out, and changing how you do things based on what you learn.

The chapter emphasizes that mastery in Python goes beyond technical prowess; it involves engaging with the community, contributing to the evolution of the language, and continuously seeking out new challenges. As you keep going, remember that the adventure isn't over yet. Python is a type of computer language that is always changing and getting new things added to it, like new tools and ways to do things. People are always finding better ways to use Python and sharing them with others. Always be curious and interested in learning new things. Keep trying to do things that are challenging and push yourself to do better and learn more.

Embrace the journey ahead with confidence and enthusiasm. The road to becoming a Python expert is paved with challenges, but it's also filled with opportunities to make a significant impact in the world of technology. Keep exploring, keep learning, and keep contributing – the future of Python is in your hands.

## Exercises: Comprehensive Capstone Projects

"Exercises: Comprehensive Capstone Projects" in the chapter "The Road Ahead: Becoming a Python Expert" are designed to be the culmination of your Python learning journey. These capstone projects integrate the knowledge and skills you've acquired, challenging you to apply them in real-world scenarios. Each project is an opportunity to demonstrate your proficiency and creativity as a Python expert.

1. **E-commerce Website with Django**: Build a fully functional e-commerce website using Django, integrating payment processing and user authentication.
2. **Stock Market Analysis Tool**: Create a Python application that analyzes stock market data in real-time, using Pandas for data manipulation and Matplotlib for data visualization.
3. **Social Media Sentiment Analysis**: Develop a tool that analyzes sentiment on social media posts using natural language processing techniques.

4. **Healthcare Data Explorer**: Create a web application that allows users to explore healthcare datasets, visualize trends, and extract insights.

5. **Automated Web Scraper and Data Analyzer**: Build a scraper that collects data from websites and analyzes it for specific patterns or anomalies.

6. **Smart Home System Simulator**: Develop a simulator for a smart home system using Python, integrating various IoT protocols.

7. **Custom Machine Learning Model for Image Recognition**: Train a machine learning model for image recognition tasks, using TensorFlow or PyTorch.

8. **Climate Change Impact Visualization Tool**: Create a tool that visualizes the impact of climate change on different regions of the world over time.

9. **Automated Resume Parser and Matcher**: Develop an application that parses resumes and matches them to job descriptions using NLP and machine learning.

10. **Personal Finance Manager with Dashboards**: Build a personal finance manager application with dashboards for expense tracking, budgeting, and forecasting.

11. **Real-Time Traffic Analysis System**: Create a system that analyzes and reports real-time traffic data, suggesting optimal routes and predicting traffic bottlenecks.

12. **Custom Content Management System (CMS)**: Design and implement a CMS with unique features, differentiating it from existing platforms.

13. **Blockchain-Based Voting System**: Develop a secure, transparent voting system using blockchain technology.

14. **Augmented Reality Educational Tool**: Create an augmented reality application for educational purposes, integrating Python with AR tools.

15. **AI Chatbot for Customer Service**: Build an AI-powered chatbot that can handle customer service inquiries efficiently.

16. **Automated Essay Grading System**: Develop a system that uses machine learning to grade essays on various criteria.

17. **Python-Powered Robotics Project**: Create a Python-controlled robot that can perform specific tasks autonomously.

18. **Cybersecurity Threat Detector**: Build a tool that detects and reports potential cybersecurity threats using Python.

19. **Genetic Algorithm for Optimization Problems**: Implement a genetic algorithm to solve complex optimization problems.

20. **Interactive Data Dashboard for Business Analytics**: Design an interactive dashboard using Plotly and Dash for business data analytics.

These capstone projects are not just tests of your Python abilities; they are a showcase of your problem-solving skills, creativity, and readiness to tackle complex challenges. As you embark on these projects, remember that they are opportunities to blend your technical knowledge with practical applications, solidifying your status as a Python expert.

# Appendix

# Python Glossary

In the dynamic world of Python programming, an array of terms and concepts form the backbone of the language, each contributing to the vast lexicon that programmers navigate daily. This glossary serves as a beacon for those traversing Python's landscape, offering clarity and insight into its fundamental elements.

**Algorithm**: In programming, there is something called an algorithm. It is like a set of instructions that helps us solve a problem by following steps one by one. In Python, algorithms transform into code, solving tasks from the simple sorting of data to complex data analysis.

**Argument**: When functions and data dance together, arguments are the special values that are given to the functions. When a function is called, arguments are the actual data pieces you specify, breathing life into the function's abstract parameters.

**Class**: Imagine a blueprint, a foundational design from which objects are created. Classes in Python are just that, defining the structure and behaviors of objects, encapsulating data and functionalities.

**Decorator**: Python's decorators are a special feature that can change how functions or methods work in a cool way. Like an artistic touch that enhances a painting, decorators wrap around a function, augmenting its execution without altering its core.

**Exception**: In Python's world, exceptions are the disruptors of normal flow, signaling that something has gone awry. Exception handling, therefore, becomes a critical practice, ensuring that these errors are gracefully caught and managed.

**Function**: These are the building blocks of Python programs, encapsulating reusable chunks of code. Defined by the `def` keyword, functions are the workhorses, performing specific tasks and often returning results.

**Generator**: Think of generators as efficient, on-demand producers of values. They allow for iteration over sequences, like lists or strings, but in a memory-efficient way, generating values one at a time and only when needed.

**Immutable**: In Python, there are some things called objects that cannot be changed once they are made. Strings and tuples are classic examples, ensuring a level of data integrity and consistency in your programs.

**Interpreter**: Python's interpreter is the engine under the hood, the translator that reads your Python code and converts it into machine-understandable instructions, executing it one line at a time.

**Lambda**: In the land of Python, lambda functions are the concise one-liners, anonymous functions defined with the lambda keyword, often used for short, throwaway functions.

**List Comprehension**: A hallmark of Python's expressiveness, list comprehensions provide a compact way of creating lists, transforming iterables with elegant and concise syntax.

**Module**: As a tapestry is formed from interwoven threads, Python modules are files of interlinked code. They encapsulate functions, classes, and variables, forming reusable components in Python programming.

**Object-Oriented Programming (OOP)**: Python embraces OOP, a paradigm centered around objects and classes, promoting code reuse and modularization. It's like organizing your toys in a way that makes them stronger, easier to use again and take care of.

**Package**: In Python, packages are directories containing modules. Like a container holding various items, they organize modules into a structured hierarchy, making code management more systematic.

**Parameter**: When defining functions, parameters are the placeholders for data. They are the variables listed in a function's definition and become meaningful when the function is called with actual arguments.

**Pythonic**: To be Pythonic is to embrace Python's philosophy, writing code that is not only syntactically correct but also adheres to its idiomatic style. It's about using Python constructs and norms effectively and elegantly.

**Recursion**: A function in Python may call itself in its definition. Recursion is like solving a big puzzle by breaking it down into smaller puzzles that are exactly the same.

**Tuple**: Among Python's data structures, tuples stand as immutable sequences. They are ordered collections, similar to lists, but their immutability makes them constant and reliable.

**Variable**: In Python, variables are like jars that have labels on them. These jars can hold different types of information. They store information which can be referenced and manipulated throughout the program.

**Zen of Python**: This is a bunch of short sayings that explain the main ideas behind how Python was made. Accessible through `import this`, it's a guiding light, a manifesto that articulates Python's core principles.

This glossary, while not exhaustive, offers a glimpse into the rich and multifaceted language that is Python. It serves as a guide, illuminating the path for both newcomers and seasoned programmers alike, as they navigate the intricate and rewarding journey of Python programming.

# Further Learning Resources

Embarking on the journey of mastering Python is akin to navigating a vast ocean; the horizon is brimming with resources, each beaconing with knowledge and new perspectives. The path to becoming a Python connoisseur is not solitary. It is enriched by a plethora of resources, communities, and tools, each offering unique insights and avenues for growth. In this segment, we explore various channels and platforms that stand as pillars of learning, guiding enthusiasts from nascent stages to the zenith of Python mastery.

### The Bedrock of Knowledge: Python Documentation

The Python documentation is the sanctum of Python's wisdom, a comprehensive and meticulously detailed resource. It is not merely a guide to Python's syntax and libraries but also an exposition of best practices and examples. The documentation is the starting point, the reference manual that provides clarity and depth, essential for both beginners and seasoned programmers.

## Online Learning Platforms: A World of Interactive Learning

The digital age has ushered in a renaissance in learning methodologies, and Python education is no exception. Websites like Coursera, Udemy, and Codecademy have lots of different classes about Python. Some classes are for beginners and some are for experts. These platforms are special because they let you learn by watching videos and doing coding activities. They make sure to teach in different ways so that everyone can learn and actually use what they learn.

## Video Tutorials: Learning in Motion

In a world where visual learning is paramount, video tutorials on platforms like YouTube present a dynamic way to learn Python. Channels managed by seasoned programmers and educators break down concepts into digestible, engaging sessions. They often cover real-world applications, making learning relatable and practical.

## Books: The Timeless Teachers

The value of books for learning Python cannot be underestimated. Books are like really detailed and organized lessons that help you learn things really well. They often teach you more than online classes do.

## Community Forums: Collective Wisdom

Platforms such as Stack Overflow and Reddit's r/learnpython are more than just Q&A sites; they are communities where learners and experts converge. They are like special pots that help us solve problems. They give us lots of information, advice, and helpful tips. Engaging with these communities can accelerate learning through real-world problem-solving and peer support.

## Podcasts: Learning on the Go

For those who find solace in auditory learning, Python podcasts like "Talk Python To Me" and "Python Bytes" offer a wealth of information. Podcasts keep you updated on the latest trends, discussions, and developments in the Python world, making learning a part of your daily routine.

## Project-Based Learning: The Practical Arena

Theory and practice go hand in hand in programming. Websites like GitHub offer a sea of open-source Python projects, ranging from simple scripts to complex applications. Contributing to these projects or even examining the code provides invaluable practical experience, a deeper understanding of how Python is used in real-world scenarios.

## Python Conferences and Meetups: Learning through Community Engagement

Conferences like PyCon and local Python meetups are not just events but congregations of Python enthusiasts and professionals. They offer workshops, talks, and networking opportunities, providing insights into Python's applications in various domains and fostering a sense of community.

## Continued Education: The Path to Specialization

For those aspiring to specialize, advanced courses and certifications are available. Topics like data science, machine learning, web development, and more can be pursued through specialized courses offered by universities and online platforms.

## Conclusion

In conclusion, the journey of learning Python is a mosaic of various resources and experiences. It is a path paved with not just code but insights, challenges, and a community ever willing to guide. As you traverse this path, remember that every resource has something unique to offer, contributing to a well-rounded understanding and mastery of Python. Keep exploring, coding, and growing; the world of Python awaits with endless possibilities.

# Acknowledgments and Contributor Notes

In the grand tapestry of this Python journey, each thread - every contribution, insight, and support - has been integral to the creation of this comprehensive guide. The tapestry is rich because of the varied hues and textures brought in by a diverse group of individuals, whose passion for Python and education shines through each page. In this section, we extend our heartfelt gratitude and acknowledge the invaluable contributions that have made this book not just a compendium of knowledge but a beacon for Python enthusiasts.

**Gratitude to the Python Community**

At the forefront of our acknowledgments is the vibrant Python community. This global congregation of enthusiasts, professionals, and pioneers has continuously pushed the boundaries of what Python can achieve. The community's commitment to open-source ideals, sharing knowledge, and fostering growth has been a guiding star. Forums, discussions, and meetups organized by this community have been a wellspring of insights and have significantly shaped the content of this book.

## Dedication of Educators and Trainers

A special note of thanks is extended to educators and trainers who have devoted their careers to teaching Python. Their resources, be it in the form of books, online courses, or interactive tutorials, have been a cornerstone in the foundational structure of this book. Their tireless efforts in simplifying complex concepts and making learning Python an engaging and enriching experience deserve our highest appreciation.

## Inspiration from Python Pioneers

We extend our respect and admiration to the pioneers of Python, especially Guido van Rossum, for envisioning and creating a language that is not only powerful and versatile but also accessible and enjoyable. Their vision has created a language that has democratized programming and opened doors for many to explore the realms of technology.

## Appreciation for Personal and Professional Support Networks

Behind every endeavor are the unsung heroes - our families, friends, and professional networks. Their cheering, helpful advice, and always being there for you have given you the energy and courage to keep going and be strong. They have been the sounding boards for ideas, the comfort in moments of challenge, and the cheerleaders celebrating every milestone.

## Final Thoughts

In conclusion, this book is not just a culmination of efforts from a few individuals but a symphony created by the collective contributions of many. Every person who has helped, whether they did it themselves or through someone else, has made a permanent impression on this project. As we acknowledge their contributions, we also celebrate the spirit of collaboration and shared learning that Python and its community embody.

We want to say thank you to everyone who has been with us on this journey. We are very grateful for your support. Your contributions, support, and faith have been the pillars upon which this guide stands. Thank you for helping me turn a vision into reality, for being part of this journey, and for continuing to inspire the Python community.

# BONUS

## ** UNLOCK YOUR GIFT BY DOWNLOADING IT NOW! **

### SIMPLY SCAN THE QR CODE PROVIDED BELOW TO ACCESS:

- Complete solutions to various exercises in the chapters.

### DIVE INTO THIS TREASURE TROVE OF RESOURCES AND ELEVATE YOUR PYTHON SKILLS!

Made in United States
Troutdale, OR
07/26/2024

21554926R10111